TM

5 STEPS TO A >> 5 =

500
AP Psychology
Questions

to know by test day

D1002957

Also in the 5 Steps series:

Also in the 500 AP Questions to Know by Test Day series:

5 STEPS TO A ➤➤ 5™

500

AP Psychology
Questions

to know by test day

THIRD EDITION

Lauren Williams
Anaxos, Inc.

New York Chicago San Francisco Athens London Madrid
Mexico City Milan New Delhi Singapore Sydney Toronto

Anaxos, Inc. has been creating education and reference materials for over fifteen years. Based in Austin, Texas, the company uses writers from across the globe who offer expertise on an array of subjects just as expansive.

1 2 3 4 5 6 7 8 9   LCR   24 23 22 21 20

ISBN   978-1-260-45975-3
MHID   1-260-45975-6

e-ISBN   978-1-260-45976-0
e-MHID   1-260-45976-4

McGraw-Hill Education products are available at special quantity discounts to use as premiums and sales promotions or for use in corporate training programs. To contact a representative, please visit the Contact Us pages at www.mhprofessional.com.

CONTENTS

INTRODUCTION

Congratulations! You've taken a big step toward AP success by purchasing *5 Steps to a 5: 500 AP Psychology Questions to Know by Test Day*. We are here to help you take the next step and score high on your AP exam so you can earn college credits and get into the college or university of your choice!

This book gives you 500 AP-style multiple-choice questions that cover all the most essential course material. Each question has a detailed answer explanation. These questions will give you valuable independent practice to supplement your regular textbook and the groundwork you are already doing in your AP classroom. This and the other books in this series were written by expert AP teachers who know your exam inside out and can identify the crucial exam information as well as questions that are most likely to appear on the exam.

You might be the kind of student who takes several AP courses and needs to study extra questions throughout the year. Or you might be the kind of student who puts off preparing until the last weeks before the exam. No matter what your preparation style, you will surely benefit from reviewing these 500 questions, which closely parallel the content, format, and degree of difficulty of the questions on the actual AP exam. These questions and their answer explanations are the ideal last-minute study tool for those final few weeks before the test.

Remember the old saying "Practice makes perfect." If you practice with all the questions and answers in this book, we are certain you will build the skills and confidence needed to do well on the exam. Good luck!

—*Editors of McGraw-Hill Education*

5 STEPS TO A >5™

500

AP Psychology
Questions

to know by test day

CHAPTER 1

Schools of Thought

1. Researchers interviewed people walking in a city square to see if they saw a colorful clown ride past them on a unicycle. They found that 75 percent of cell phone users did not recall seeing the clown while more than 50 percent of non-cell users saw the clown. The study fits into which field of psychology?

(A) Cognitive
(B) Social
(C) Personality
(D) Learning
(E) Perception

2. Which school of thought was established by Wilhelm Wundt and his student Edward Bradford Titchener and focused on looking inward to discover how the mind was composed?

(A) Humanistic psychology
(B) Functionalism
(C) Structuralism
(D) Behaviorism
(E) Empiricism

3. "The basic thesis of gestalt theory might be formulated thus: there are contexts in which what is happening in the whole cannot be deduced from characteristics of the separate process, but conversely, what happens to a part of the whole is, in clear-cut cases, determined by the laws of the inner structure of the whole." Who most likely stated this?

(A) John Watson
(B) William James
(C) Ivan Pavlov
(D) Max Wertheimer
(E) Sigmund Freud

4. Which of the following psychologists wrote *The Principles of Psychology*?
   (A) William James
   (B) Wilhelm Wundt
   (C) John Watson
   (D) Sigmund Freud
   (E) Max Wertheimer

5. Psychology is considered a science mainly because it relies on direct observation. Which field of psychology supports this?
   (A) Behaviorism
   (B) Psychodynamic psychology
   (C) Social psychology
   (D) Cognitive psychology
   (E) Structuralism

6. A psychologist is treating her patient with a combination of antidepressants and psychotherapy. Which of the following best describes this approach?
   (A) Cognitive psychology
   (B) Psychodynamic psychology
   (C) Social psychology
   (D) Eclectic psychology
   (E) Counseling psychology

7. Psychoanalytic psychology focuses mainly on:
   (A) Rewards and punishments
   (B) Self-esteem and self-actualization
   (C) Biology and genetics
   (D) Internal conflict and unconscious desires
   (E) Sensation and perception

8. One major criticism of Ivan Pavlov's concept of classical conditioning was that:
   (A) It did not take into account voluntary human behavior.
   (B) It was unethical to use dogs in a psychology experiment.
   (C) It did not take into account involuntary behavior.
   (D) The findings overlapped with other fields of psychology.
   (E) It did not differentiate between a conditioned and an unconditioned stimulus.

9. Which of the following psychologists was influenced by Charles Darwin and promoted a school of thought that focused on the sway of evolutionary adaptation on cognitive and behavioral processes?
   (A) John Watson
   (B) William James
   (C) Wilhelm Wundt
   (D) Max Wertheimer
   (E) Sigmund Freud

10. The use of rewards, punishments, and positive reinforcement is an example of which field of psychology?
    (A) Personality
    (B) Behavioral
    (C) Social
    (D) Cognitive
    (E) Psychoanalytic

11. "Give me a dozen healthy infants and my own special world to bring them up in, and I'll guarantee to take any one at random and train him to become any type of specialist, . . . lawyer, doctor. . . ." What psychological approach would support this statement?
    (A) Cognitive
    (B) Structural
    (C) Functional
    (D) Behavioral
    (E) Psychoanalytic

12. How did behaviorism, developed by B. F. Skinner and John B. Watson, redefine psychology in the first half of the twentieth century?
    (A) Behaviorism applied concepts from evolutionary biology to psychology.
    (B) Behaviorism focused on the scientific study of objective, observable actions.
    (C) Behaviorism emphasized self-reflection as a means to study the human mind.
    (D) Behaviorism focused on bringing attention to the unconscious mind.
    (E) Behaviorism used early childhood memories and learned conditioned responses to understand human behavior.

13. One major difference between structuralism and functionalism is:

(A) Structuralists analyze all mental elements, while functionalists analyze only some elements.

(B) Structuralists believe all behaviors stem from the evolutionary process.

(C) Structuralists wish to divide the mind into mental elements while functionalists believe behavior helps an organism adapt to the environment.

(D) Only functionalists believe in the importance of introspection.

(E) Structuralists try to manipulate the mind in order to understand behavior, while functionalists study the conscious mind to understand behavior.

14. The idea that psychology is *not* based on scientific fact or human shortcomings but instead should focus on human experience is the basis for which psychological approach?

(A) Cognitive psychology

(B) Structuralism

(C) Behaviorism

(D) Functionalism

(E) Humanism

15. Clients who work with their therapists to explore their unconscious to discover the source of their illness would be seeking what type of therapy?

(A) Psychoanalytic

(B) Humanist

(C) Cognitive

(D) Eclectic

(E) Behavioral

16. Psychodynamic psychology focuses mainly on which of the following?

(A) Free will and self-actualization

(B) Experiments in controlled settings

(C) The collective unconscious

(D) Thoughts, impulses, and desires beyond the conscious being

(E) Practical introspection

17. A developmental psychologist focuses mainly on:

(A) The conscious experiences of an infant

(B) The manner in which a child develops the ability to speak, learn, and understand the world around him or her

(C) The mental process that helps a young person adapt to his or her environment

(D) The identification of one's environment and response to the environment

(E) Experiments that emphasize actual behavior, rather than controlled settings

18. A psychology researcher studying how problem solving and memory is affected by frequent distraction is most likely practicing:

(A) Cognitive psychology

(B) Social-cultural psychology

(C) Evolutionary psychology

(D) Psychodynamic psychology

(E) Behavioral psychology

19. A scientist is studying the role of serotonin in anxiety and depression. Which area of psychology is the scientist most likely practicing?

(A) Clinical psychology

(B) Cognitive psychology

(C) Biological psychology

(D) Comparative psychology

(E) Health psychology

20. A case study is:

(A) A primary tool for investigation into a client's unconscious through dream analysis and free association

(B) A study done over an entire life span of one individual, giving the psychologist detailed information of one's psyche

(C) A study that exposes the subject to some event and measures coping skills

(D) An independent study used outside the natural environment of the subject

(E) A comparative study of various people of different ages at the same time

CHAPTER 2

Research Methods

21. A study found evidence that married people have a better chance of surviving cancer than do single people, meaning that the unmarried people might be good targets for cancer-prevention programs. Which of the following best describes this type of research?

(A) Experimental research
(B) Surveys
(C) Case studies
(D) Correlational research
(E) Naturalistic observations

22. A random sample can best be defined as:

(A) A sample in which each potential participant has an equal chance of being selected
(B) A sample that is carefully chosen so the characteristics of participants correspond to the larger population
(C) A selection of cases from a larger population
(D) A selection of cases from the control group
(E) A sample of a larger population from the experimental group

23. The Hawthorne effect is best defined as:

(A) Expectations by the experimenter that can influence the results of an experiment
(B) The change in the results of an experiment when it is "blind" versus "double blind"
(C) The idea that people will alter their behavior because of the researchers' attention and not because of actual treatment
(D) Specific, testable predictions derived from a theory
(E) The idea that subjects in an experiment will lie if the researcher tells them to

24. Dr. Bisell conducts an experiment to see whether hunger makes mice run faster through a maze. He randomly assigns 25 mice to a control group or an experimental group. Which cannot be a confounding variable?

(A) Where the experiment takes place
(B) How hungry the mice were before the experiment
(C) How fast the mice are before the race
(D) When the experiment takes place
(E) The population from which he selected the mice

25. Marc, a psychology major, collected survey data about the number of hours that college students study for finals and their grades on those finals. His data indicate that students who spend more time studying for finals tend to do better than other students. What can Marc now conclude?

(A) Studying improves a student's grade on a final exam.
(B) A relationship exists between studying and exam grades.
(C) A significant relationship exists between studying and grades.
(D) Students who do not study for final exams will not do well on those exams.
(E) Students with higher IQs tend to study more than those with lower IQs.

26. Jordan runs an experiment testing the effects of sugar consumption on aggression levels in children. He randomly assigns 20 subjects either to a control group given sugar-free candy or to the experimental group that was given the same candy that did contain sugar. He then tests the subjects' response to several different puzzles, each with increasing difficulty. Jordan hypothesizes that sugar levels do play a role in aggression in children. In order to know whether his hypothesis has been supported, Jordan will need to use:

(A) Descriptive statistics
(B) Means-to-end statistics
(C) Experimental research
(D) Scatter plots
(E) Inferential statistics

27. Which of the following coefficients of a correlation indicates the weakest relationship between sleep habits and grades?
    (A) 0.51
    (B) −0.28
    (C) 0.08
    (D) −1.00
    (E) 1.00

28. After evaluating several experimental groups using a math test, a researcher is working with the following three sets of test scores: [0, 0, 14, 14], [0, 6, 8, 14], and [6, 6, 8, 8]. All of the data sets have the same mean of 7. Which data set is most likely to have the largest standard deviation?
    (A) [0, 0, 14, 14]
    (B) [0, 6, 8, 14]
    (C) [6, 6, 8, 8]
    (D) All of the data sets are likely to have the same standard deviation.
    (E) [0, 0, 14, 14] and [6, 6, 8, 8] are likely to have the same standard deviation.

29. In an experiment, Sydney is going to investigate how alcohol affects aggression. The number of alcoholic drinks the subject has is called the:
    (A) Controlled variable
    (B) Independent variable
    (C) Dependent variable
    (D) Experimental variable
    (E) Positive variable

30. Height tends to fall on a normal distribution. The average height for an adult male in the United States is 70 inches. With a standard deviation of 3 inches, approximately what proportion of men in the United States are taller than 79 inches?
    (A) 34   percent
    (B) 15.6 percent
    (C) 13.5 percent
    (D) 2   percent
    (E) 0.1 percent

31. In a statistical study of the effectiveness of two drugs for treating depression, researchers reported treatment A "provided statistically significant better results for depression" than treatment B. Which of the following most likely can be assumed?

(A) It is proven that subjects taking drug A will have a clinically significant improvement.

(B) There is no possibility of bias in the study.

(C) Effect is large enough to seem unlikely to have occurred solely by chance.

(D) There is a practical significance that is important.

(E) Drug A is probably more effective than drug B.

32. IQ tests scores were compared between schools A and B. School B had a positive Z score while school A had a negative Z score. These scores definitively show:

(A) Children at school A are not as intelligent as children at school B.

(B) Children at school B scored above the mean.

(C) The IQ test result differences are statistically significant between the two schools.

(D) Children at school B are above average in intelligence.

(E) None of the above.

33. For a normal distribution, approximately what percentage of the data points should fall within two standard deviations above or below the mean?

(A) 2 percent

(B) 13.5 percent

(C) 34 percent

(D) 68 percent

(E) 95 percent

34. In a history class, students received their scores from a test. This test was particularly challenging, and the average test score was 70 percent. However, few students received a score close to 70 percent. Many students were well prepared and managed to score above 85 percent, but a significant number of students did not prepare well and received failing grades, dragging the class average down. What type of distribution is this?

(A) Normal distribution
(B) Standard distribution
(C) Median distribution
(D) Skewed distribution
(E) Differential distribution

35. Which of the following is *not* a part of the scientific method?

(A) Forming a theory based on observable facts
(B) Creating a hypothesis to test a prediction implied by a theory
(C) Testing a hypothesis using research and observations
(D) Searching for results that confirm the hypothesis
(E) Revising the initial theory based on the conclusions drawn from research and observations

36. Jack wants to study the behavior of cats. He sets up a camera in his house to record his cat throughout the day. At the end of each day, he watches the recordings and takes detailed notes about his cat's behavioral patterns. What type of method is Jack using?

(A) Naturalistic observation
(B) A survey study
(C) An experiment
(D) A correlational study
(E) A double-blind study

37. Which of the following is a reason why science-based methods are more valid than intuition and common sense?

(A) People tend to be overconfident in their knowledge, regardless of its accuracy.
(B) People tend to find order and patterns even in random events.
(C) People tend to believe, after learning of an outcome, that they could have predicted it.
(D) All of the above.
(E) None of the above.

38. Three friends want to bet on a horse race. One of the friends decides to go against the grain and chooses the horse with the lowest odds of winning the race, saying he "has a good feeling about this horse." Despite the low odds, his horse wins the race. He then claims he was certain his horse would win from the beginning. Which concept is this an example of?

    (A) Sampling bias
    (B) Hindsight bias
    (C) Confirmation bias
    (D) Selection bias
    (E) Bandwagon effect

39. A survey study on the patterns of illicit drug use among teenagers includes participants from high schools across the United States. However, the study fails to include adolescents who have dropped out of high school or are home-schooled. What is this an example of?

    (A) Sampling bias
    (B) Hindsight bias
    (C) Confirmation bias
    (D) Selection bias
    (E) Bandwagon effect

40. Lisa is testing whether caffeine will influence heart rate. She recruits students with an advertisement. She splits the participants into two groups, one male and one female. Lisa has a friend randomly administer regular coffee or decaf coffee to each group without Lisa knowing which group received which beverage. Lisa then measures their heart rates. Which factor represents a weakness in Lisa's experimental design?

    (A) This is a descriptive study, not an experiment.
    (B) She does not have a random sample of the population.
    (C) She does not use a double-blind procedure.
    (D) The experimental and control groups were not randomly assigned.
    (E) Both B and D.

CHAPTER 3

The Brain

41. A relative has been in a serious car accident and the doctor informs the family that the reticular formation part of the brain has been severely damaged. She tells the family that their relative will likely:

(A) Have speech and language issues
(B) Have motivational and emotional issues
(C) Have sensory motor issues
(D) Be irritable, sad, and depressed
(E) Be in a state of permanent unconsciousness

42. An EEG records:

(A) Direct electrical stimulation of the brain
(B) The number of neurons in the brain
(C) Electrical impulses from the brain
(D) Chemical activity in specific areas of the brain
(E) Stimulation of the frontal lobe

43. Mary had a split-brain operation to treat her epilepsy. However, ever since the operation she has had difficulty choosing the correct groceries from the supermarket shelf. Which part of her brain has been affected?

(A) Cerebellum
(B) Corpus callosum
(C) Cerebrum
(D) Medulla
(E) Pons

Use the diagram of a brain below to answer the following questions.

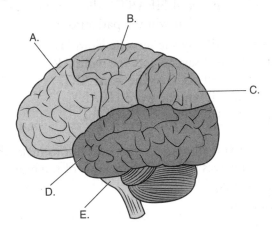

53. Which labeled area or areas in the diagram make up the cerebral cortex of the brain?

    (A) Region A
    (B) Regions A and B
    (C) Regions B and C
    (D) Regions A, B, C, and D
    (E) Regions A, B, C, D, and E

54. Which of the labeled areas in the diagram is important for speech, muscle movement, planning, and decision making?

    (A) Region A
    (B) Region B
    (C) Region C
    (D) Region D
    (E) Region E

55. Which of the labeled areas in the diagram contains the motor cortex?

    (A) Region A
    (B) Region B
    (C) Region C
    (D) Region D
    (E) Region E

56. Which of the labeled areas in the diagram contains the area that controls hearing?

(A) Region A
(B) Region B
(C) Region C
(D) Region D
(E) Region E

57. Which of the labeled areas in the diagram controls heartbeat and breathing and represents the oldest region of the brain?

(A) Region A
(B) Region B
(C) Region C
(D) Region D
(E) Region E

CHAPTER 4

Neuroscience

Use the diagram below of a neuron to answer the following questions.

58. Which of the labeled areas in the diagram acts as the life support center?

   (A) Region A
   (B) Region B
   (C) Region C
   (D) Region D
   (E) Region E

59. Which of the labeled areas in the diagram represents the myelin sheath?

   (A) Region A
   (B) Region B
   (C) Region C
   (D) Region D
   (E) Region E

60. Which of the labeled areas in the diagram represents the extensions that pass messages from the cell body?

(A) Region A
(B) Region B
(C) Region C
(D) Region D
(E) Region E

61. Which of the labeled areas in the diagram receives messages from other cells?

(A) Region A
(B) Region B
(C) Region C
(D) Region D
(E) Region E

62. Which of the labeled areas in the diagram interacts with and sends messages to neighboring cells?

(A) Region A
(B) Region B
(C) Region C
(D) Region D
(E) Region E

63. If an action potential starts at the beginning of an axon, the action potential will continue at the same speed to the very end of the axon. This concept is known as:

(A) Nerve impulse
(B) Synapse
(C) Resting state
(D) All-or-none law
(E) Sodium pump

64. Which of the following functions best explains the role of the sympathetic nervous system?

(A) Preparing the body for a traumatic event
(B) Returning the body to equilibrium
(C) Preparing the body for "fight or flight"
(D) Maintaining the body's vital functions
(E) Maintaining homeostasis

65. Which of the following neurotransmitters most closely resembles the effects alcohol has on the nervous system?

(A) Anandamide
(B) GABA
(C) Dopamine
(D) Acetylcholine
(E) Serotonin

66. What is one major difference between the sympathetic and parasympathetic nervous systems?

(A) The sympathetic nervous system increases physiological arousal, while the parasympathetic nervous system returns the body to a calmer and relaxed state.
(B) The sympathetic nervous system is a subdivision of the somatic nervous system, while the parasympathetic nervous system is a subdivision of the autonomic nervous system.
(C) The sympathetic nervous system plays a role in traumatic events, while the parasympathetic nervous system only plays a role in digestion.
(D) The parasympathetic nervous system is used more often than the sympathetic nervous system.
(E) The sympathetic nervous system plays a role in sexual behavior, while the parasympathetic nervous system does not.

67. Neurons that carry information away from the spinal cord to produce responses in various muscles or organs throughout the body are called:

(A) Afferent neurons
(B) Interneurons
(C) Neurotransmitters
(D) Sensor neurons
(E) Efferent neurons

68. Many neurotransmitters play multiple roles in the brain and the body. For example, one neurotransmitter plays a role in learning and memory while also helping our muscles communicate with the central nervous system. Which neurotransmitter does this describe?

(A) Serotonin
(B) GABA
(C) Glutamate
(D) Dopamine
(E) Acetylcholine

69. Dopamine is a neurotransmitter that affects movement, learning, attention, and emotion. Which disease can result if the body's supply of dopamine becomes too low?

(A) Schizophrenia
(B) Parkinson's disease
(C) Depression
(D) Alzheimer's disease
(E) Huntington's disease

70. Which of the following acts as the body's major inhibitory neurotransmitter?

(A) Serotonin
(B) GABA
(C) Glutamate
(D) Dopamine
(E) Acetylcholine

71. Opiate drugs act by mimicking the effects of certain types of naturally occurring neurotransmitters. Opiate drugs are similar enough in structure that they can bind to the same receptors in the brain. This produces a temporary high by activating the normal pathways that yield feelings of pleasure. Drugs that can bind to receptors in the brain and elicit a response are called:

(A) Agonists
(B) Endorphins
(C) Antagonists
(D) Protagonists
(E) Mimetics

72. Scientists used to believe that the ends of individual neurons fused together to create an uninterrupted fabric. However, British physiologist Sir Charles Sherrington noticed that neural impulses took longer than expected to travel between neurons. He predicted there must be a brief interruption in transmission. What did Sherrington name the meeting point between two neurons?

(A) Axon
(B) Action potential
(C) Synapse
(D) Receptor
(E) Dendritic cleft

CHAPTER 5

Sensation and Perception

73. According to the cocktail party effect, we can only focus on one voice at a time while in a crowded room with many people talking. This is an example of:

(A) Selective attention
(B) Top-down processing
(C) Bottom-up processing
(D) Selective inattention
(E) Priming

74. Taste: 1 gram of table salt in 500 liters of water; smell: 1 drop of perfume diffused throughout a three-room apartment; touch: the wing of a bee falling on your cheek from a height of 1 centimeter away. These are all examples of:

(A) The just-noticeable difference of our senses
(B) The difference threshold for our senses
(C) The absolute threshold of our senses
(D) The adaptation of our senses
(E) The perception of our senses

75. Weber's law can best be defined as:

(A) The smallest change in stimulation that can be detected 50 percent of the time
(B) The principle that the just-noticeable difference for any given sense is a constant proportion of the stimulation being judged
(C) The principle that there is an adjustment of sensation levels depending on the stimulation received
(D) The idea that the least amount of energy detected in a stimulation only occurs 50 percent of the time
(E) The theory that all stimuli respond to the same sensations through the process of creating meaningful patterns

76. The name of the transparent protective coating over the front part of the eye is:

(A) Lens
(B) Iris
(C) Pupil
(D) Fovea
(E) Cornea

77. The function of the lens is to:

(A) Project an image onto the cornea
(B) Focus an image on the retina
(C) Locate an image
(D) Contain receptor cells that are sensitive to light
(E) Locate the blind spot

78. An afterimage can best be defined as:

(A) Sense experience that occurs after a visual stimulus has been removed
(B) Decreased sensitivity of rods and cones in bright light
(C) Increased sensitivity of rods and cones in darkness
(D) Distinguishable fine details of a stimulation
(E) Nondistinguishable details of a stimulation

79. The theory of color that best explains color afterimage is:

(A) The volley theory
(B) The trichromatic theory
(C) The opponent-process theory
(D) The subtractive color theory
(E) The monochromatic theory

80. Trichromats can mix which three colors to perceive virtually any hue?

(A) Red, blue, green
(B) Red, blue, yellow
(C) Blue, yellow, green
(D) Red, green, yellow
(E) Yellow, orange, green

81. Which type of hearing loss is caused by damage to the mechanical system that conducts sound waves to the cochlea?

(A) Sensorineural hearing loss
(B) Conduction hearing loss
(C) Nerve deafness
(D) Threshold hearing loss
(E) Inner ear deafness

82. When the molecules of a skunk's spray enter your nose, the molecules are transformed into electrical signals, or impulses, that are interpreted by the brain as an unpleasant odor. This is an example of:

(A) Adaptation
(B) Transduction
(C) Sensation
(D) Perception
(E) Stimulation

83. While driving home in a bad storm, you remain highly focused on the road ahead to avoid an accident. When you get home, you turn on the news and realize you passed the aftermath of a severe accident on your drive. However, you were so focused on driving safely that you did not notice it at the time. This is an example of:

(A) Selective attention
(B) Top-down processing
(C) Bottom-up processing
(D) Selective inattention
(E) Priming

84. Frequency is to _____ as amplitude is to _____.

(A) sensation; perception
(B) loudness; pitch
(C) pitch; loudness
(D) perception; sensation
(E) warmth; cold

85. Olfactory cells are the receptors for what sense?

(A) Taste
(B) Hearing
(C) Vision
(D) Smell
(E) Touch

86. The binocular cue for depth perception based on signals from muscles that turn the eyes to focus on near or approaching objects is called:

(A) Convergence
(B) Retinal disparity
(C) Shape constancy
(D) Interposition
(E) Perceptual vision

87. As a car drives away, it projects a smaller and smaller image on your retina. Although the retinal image grows smaller, you do *not* perceive the car as shrinking because of:

(A) Shape constancy
(B) Size continuity
(C) Size constancy
(D) Shape continuity
(E) Size perception

88. Which of the following is *not* a monocular depth cue?

(A) Linear perspective
(B) Interposition
(C) Relative size
(D) Texture gradient
(E) Convergence

89. The final step required to convert vibrations into sound sensations takes place in which part of the ear?

(A) Ossicles
(B) Outer ear
(C) Cochlea
(D) Middle ear
(E) Auditory receptors

90. Which of the following statements best defines the gate control theory of pain?

(A) Pain impulses are sent to receptor sites in vital organs.

(B) Nonpainful nerve impulses compete with pain impulses to reach the brain, creating a neural blockage and reducing pain.

(C) Stimuli of various kinds activate free nerve endings.

(D) Pain is simply a psychological state, not a physiological one.

(E) Perception of pain depends on one's physical makeup.

91. Black-and-white vision with greatest sensitivity under low levels of illumination describes the role of:

(A) The cones

(B) The cornea

(C) The fovea

(D) The rods

(E) The pupil

92. The distinction between top-down and bottom-up effects plays a central role in experimental psychology. The following is an example of bottom-up processing:

(A) Jimmy is putting a puzzle together without a picture of the finished product.

(B) Johnny keeps his hands away from the hot stove after burning his hand once before.

(C) Jimmy is putting a puzzle together following a picture he has of the finished product.

(D) Johnny is sitting too close to a campfire but quickly moves away when his leg begins to get too hot.

(E) James is driving down the street looking for a convenience store and sees a sign with several missing letters but guesses that this is the entrance to the store.

93. The following is an example of Jane using top-down processing:

(A) Using phonetics to sound out a word

(B) Piecing a puzzle together by looking at the puzzle without a picture

(C) Making your way through an unlighted maze from the inside without a flashlight

(D) Understanding difficult handwriting when placed in the context of complete sentences

(E) Instant feeling of fear in response to a car pulling out in front of you

94. Sensation is the neurological process by which we become aware of our environment. You are at a crowded and noisy party and are trying to focus on the conversation you are having with a friend. Your ability to do this while mostly ignoring the flood of other information coming into your senses is known as:

(A) Absolute threshold

(B) Difference threshold

(C) Signal detection

(D) Sensory adaptation

(E) Maintaining perceptual constancy

95. Which of the following properties of light is determined by wavelength?

(A) Hue

(B) Intensity

(C) Visibility

(D) A and B

(E) A and C

96. Specialized neurons in the visual cortex respond to the specific characteristics of visual input such as shape, angle, or movement. What are these neurons called?

(A) Rod cells

(B) Input detectors

(C) Cone cells

(D) Feature detectors

(E) Optical nerves

97. In the study of hearing, this theory explains that the rate of nerve impulses traveling up the auditory nerve is what allows us to decipher pitch. This theory is referred to as:

(A) The place theory
(B) The parallel processing theory
(C) The signal detection theory
(D) Weber's theory
(E) The frequency theory

98. Which of the following food characteristic is indicated by a sweet taste?

(A) Sodium essential to physiological processes
(B) Energy source
(C) Potentially toxic acid
(D) Potential poison
(E) Proteins to grow and repair tissue

CHAPTER 6

Consciousness, Sleep, and Dreams

99. Driving a car along a familiar route while listening to the radio or thinking of something else is an example of:

(A) Automatic process
(B) Controlled process
(C) Somatic process
(D) Sympathetic process
(E) Parasympathetic process

100. When researchers removed all time cues, such as light, clock, radio, and television, from subjects' environment, the length of the day expanded from 24 to about 25 hours. This phenomenon is known as:

(A) The interval timing clock
(B) The circadian rhythm
(C) The biological clock
(D) The internal rhythm
(E) The external clock

101. The hormone most closely related to one's sleep patterns is:

(A) Serotonin
(B) Norepinephrine
(C) Epinephrine
(D) Melatonin
(E) Dopamine

102. Which stage of sleep is characterized by delta waves (very high amplitude and very low frequency)?

    (A) Non-REM stage 3 sleep
    (B) Non-REM stage 2 sleep
    (C) Non-REM stage 1 sleep
    (D) REM sleep
    (E) Non-REM stage 3 sleep and REM sleep

103. When in this stage of sleep, brain waves have a fast frequency and low amplitude, and they look very similar to beta waves, which occur when you are wide awake and alert. Which state of sleep is this?

    (A) Non-REM stage 1 sleep
    (B) Non-REM stage 2 sleep
    (C) Non-REM stage 3 sleep
    (D) REM sleep
    (E) Non-REM stage 1 sleep and REM sleep

104. Sleepwalking and sleep talking are characteristics of which stage of sleep?

    (A) REM sleep
    (B) Non-REM stage 1 sleep
    (C) Non-REM stage 2 sleep
    (D) Non-REM stage 3 sleep
    (E) REM sleep and non-REM stage 3 sleep

105. An infant sleeps approximately 17 hours a day. Of those hours, how many are spent in REM?

    (A) 20 percent
    (B) 30 percent
    (C) 50 percent
    (D) 70 percent
    (E) 80 percent

106. The adaptive sleep theory suggests:

(A) Daily activities deplete key factors in our brain and body that are replenished by sleep.

(B) Sleep evolved because it prevented early humans and animals from wasting energy and exposing themselves to dangers of nocturnal predators.

(C) For our internal clocks to have synchrony with the external world, thereby decreasing fatigue, disorientation, and lack of concentration, sleep is necessary.

(D) Sleep is necessary to combat insomnia and drowsiness.

(E) External environments are constantly competing with individual sleep rhythms. Sleep is necessary to compete with the external clock.

107. The center of the activation-synthesis hypothesis of dreaming is based on the belief that:

(A) The conscious needs to express unfulfilled wishes.

(B) Dreams provide an outlet for repressed thoughts.

(C) Dreams are the result of physiological activity in the brain.

(D) The unconscious needs to exhibit socially unacceptable behavior.

(E) Dreams allow the individual to work out daily hassles.

108. The idea that dreams represent wish fulfillment comes from which theory of dream interpretation?

(A) Extension of waking life

(B) Activation synthesis

(C) Spiritual world

(D) Transformation dream analysis

(E) Freud's theory of dream interpretation

109. Repeated periods during sleep when a person stops breathing for 10 seconds or longer is known as:

(A) Narcolepsy

(B) Sleep apnea

(C) Sleep agnosia

(D) Insomnia

(E) Night terrors

110. A person experiences blind panic, screaming, and thrashing around while sleeping. This episode is called:

(A) A night terror
(B) A nightmare
(C) A sleep terror
(D) Dreaming
(E) A REM rebound episode

111. A relatively rare condition that involves irresistible attacks of sleepiness, brief periods of REM, and often muscle paralysis is called:

(A) Sleep apnea
(B) Sleep terror
(C) Narcolepsy
(D) Benzodiazepines
(E) Night terror

112. REM sleep is also known as paradoxical sleep because:

(A) Measures of the brain activity closely resemble waking consciousness, but the person is in the deepest stage of sleep.
(B) Measures of the brain activity closely resemble waking consciousness, but the person is incapable of moving.
(C) The person's heart rate is slower than when awake, but the person can sleepwalk or sleep talk.
(D) The person can have night terrors during this stage but will not remember them in the morning.
(E) The person's vital signs are very slow, but the person can get up and walk around.

113. James has been taken to the hospital after being violently attacked. The hospital staff decides to keep James awake as long as possible to help ease the psychological trauma and erase the unpleasant experiences from memory. This is an example of which theory of dreams?

(A) Activation synthesis
(B) Reverse learning
(C) Psychoanalytic
(D) Lucid dreaming
(E) Continual-activation

114. Alteration in consciousness that occurs seemingly without effort, typically when we want to momentarily escape reality, is called:

(A) Daydreaming
(B) Dreaming
(C) Meditation
(D) Hypnosis
(E) Anesthesia

115. A sleep disorder characterized by difficulty in falling asleep or remaining asleep is called:

(A) Narcolepsy
(B) Sleep apnea
(C) Insomnia
(D) Sleep terror
(E) Nightmares

116. Which of the following is *not* a characteristic of REM sleep?

(A) Rapid eye movement
(B) Vivid dreams
(C) Increased heart rate
(D) Paralysis
(E) Delta waves

117. Approximately how many cycles of sleep does an adult enter during a full night's sleep?

(A) One to two
(B) Three to four
(C) Four to five
(D) Six to seven
(E) Seven to eight

118. Approximately how long is each cycle of sleep during a full night's sleep?

(A) 80 minutes
(B) 90 minutes
(C) 60 minutes
(D) 70 minutes
(E) 50 minutes

119. Experimenters have shown that a person deprived of the
_____ stage of sleep will become anxious, testy, and hungry
and have difficulty concentrating.

(A) REM sleep
(B) Non-REM stage 1 sleep
(C) Non-REM stage 2 sleep
(D) Non-REM stage 3 sleep
(E) REM sleep and non-REM stage 3 sleep

120. Before entering sleep, you briefly pass through a relaxed and drowsy
state. This is marked by which characteristic?

(A) Beta waves
(B) Delta waves
(C) Alpha waves
(D) Theta waves
(E) Zeta waves

121. Which part of the brain is important in keeping the forebrain alert
and producing a state of wakefulness?

(A) Hippocampus
(B) Limbic system
(C) Hindbrain
(D) Reticular formation
(E) Medulla

122. The dream theory that suggests our dreams reflect the same
thoughts, fears, and concerns present when we are awake is called:

(A) Freud's theory of dreams
(B) Extension of waking life
(C) Activation-synthesis
(D) External world
(E) Spiritual world

123. Eighty percent of our sleep takes place in which cycle of sleep?

(A) REM sleep
(B) Non-REM stage 1 sleep
(C) Non-REM stage 2 sleep
(D) Non-REM stage 3 sleep
(E) Stages 1, 2, and 3 of non-REM sleep

124. Beta waves are characteristic of a person who is:

(A) Dreaming

(B) In a coma

(C) Asleep but not dreaming

(D) Awake and alert

(E) In stage 1 sleep

125. _____ refers to an increased percentage of time spent in REM sleep when we are deprived of REM sleep on the previous night.

(A) REM rebound

(B) REM deprivation

(C) REM sleep

(D) REM makeup

(E) REM extension

CHAPTER 7

Drugs and Hypnosis

126. According to Ernest Hilgard's hidden observer theory, people who are hypnotized and told to plunge one hand into a glass of painfully cold ice water with the suggestion they will not feel pain, will respond to the question "Do you feel pain?" by:

(A) Saying they do not feel pain
(B) Waking up from the hypnotic trance
(C) Screaming and removing their hand from the water
(D) Screaming but leaving their hand in the water
(E) Saying they do feel pain

127. Which of these does *not* describe a symptom of a drug-use disorder?

(A) Trying unsuccessfully to regulate substance use
(B) Continuing use despite hazards
(C) Experiencing withdrawal when attempting to end use
(D) Using to impress peers or gain access to a social group
(E) Disrupting obligations at work, school, or home

128. Which statement best defines dependency?

(A) The original dosage of the drug no longer produces desired effects.
(B) Behavioral patterns are marked by overwhelming desire to obtain and use the drug.
(C) A change in the nervous system occurs so that a person now needs to take the drug to prevent withdrawal symptoms.
(D) Painful physical and psychological symptoms occur after the drug is no longer in the system.
(E) Decompression from the peripheral nervous system begins after the drug enters the body.

129. Which of the following drugs blocks reuptake, leading to increased neural stimulation?

(A) Heroin
(B) Cocaine
(C) Morphine
(D) Amphetamines
(E) Methamphetamines

130. Which of the following drugs does *not* fall under the category of a stimulant?

(A) Cocaine
(B) Caffeine
(C) Nicotine
(D) Amphetamines
(E) Heroin

131. The reduction in the body's response to a drug, which may accompany continual drug use, is called:

(A) Withdrawal
(B) Addiction
(C) Dependency
(D) Tolerance
(E) Hallucinations

132. This drug depresses neural functioning. As a result, the user's breathing slows, pupils constrict, and a blissful feeling of pleasure replaces all feelings of pain and anxiety. However, tolerance quickly develops, requiring larger and larger doses to feel the same effects. Users risk overdose from increasingly large doses, and extreme withdrawal symptoms occur if use of the drug is ceased. Which drug does this describe?

(A) Cocaine
(B) Nicotine
(C) Heroin
(D) LSD
(E) Psilocybin

133. Hallucinogens are best defined as:

(A) Psychoactive drugs that produce strange and unusual perceptual, sensory, and cognitive experiences

(B) Stimulants that produce arousals both physically and psychologically

(C) Designer drugs that cause three primary effects: pain reduction, euphoria, and tolerance

(D) Mild depressants that decrease heart rate and blood pressure

(E) Drugs that stimulate the central nervous system

134. In order for a person to be hypnotized, the hypnotist must do which of the following?

(A) Suggest what the subject will experience during hypnosis.

(B) Tell the subject what he or she will be doing while under hypnosis.

(C) Tell the subject to count from 10 to 1.

(D) Suggest that the subject enter a trance.

(E) Tell the subject to relax and feel no stress.

135. Slowed neural processing, reduced self-awareness and self-control, memory disruption, and the expectancy effect are all effects of which drug?

(A) LSD

(B) Cocaine

(C) Alcohol

(D) Barbiturates

(E) Heroin

136. _____ are psychoactive drugs that depress the central nervous system, while _____ stimulate the central nervous system.

(A) Opiates, barbiturates

(B) Opiates, amphetamines

(C) Barbiturates, amphetamines

(D) Amphetamines, barbiturates

(E) Amphetamines, opiates

137. What are the four major areas of impact of psychoactive drugs?

(A) Appetite, behavior, sex drive, perception
(B) Perception, behavior, moods, mental processes
(C) Perception, mental processes, appetite, digestion
(D) Appetite, perception, moods, mental processes
(E) Mental processes, moods, digestion, perception

138. Which of the following psychoactive drugs is *not* a depressant?

(A) Alcohol
(B) Barbiturates
(C) Benzodiazepines
(D) Heroin
(E) Nembutal

139. This drug induces a number of physiological and psychological effects, some of which include dilated blood vessels in the eye, dry mouth, time distortion, euphoric feelings, sense of relaxation, and mild muscular weakness.

(A) Alcohol
(B) Marijuana
(C) LSD
(D) Tranquilizers
(E) Cocaine

140. Which of the following is *not* a practical application of hypnosis?

(A) Ease pain
(B) Stop smoking
(C) Remember a painful event
(D) Stop overeating
(E) Marriage counseling

141. In the 1700s a force called "animal magnetism," later known as hypnosis, was introduced by:

(A) Sigmund Freud
(B) Ernest Hilgard
(C) Wilhelm Wundt
(D) William James
(E) Anton Mesmer

142. In using hypnosis for pain reduction, patients highly susceptible to hypnosis were:

(A) More likely to experience posthypnotic amnesia
(B) Less likely to participate in future studies
(C) More likely to report significantly lower pain levels
(D) Less likely to report lower pain levels
(E) Likely to respond more slowly to the induction method

143. All of the following are terms related to hypnosis except:

(A) Posthypnotic amnesia
(B) Hidden observer
(C) Suggestibility
(D) Hypnotic analgesia
(E) Posthypnotic exhortation

CHAPTER 8

Classical Conditioning

144. A group of ranchers attempts to discourage coyotes from attacking their sheep by placing a substance on the wool of the sheep that makes coyotes violently ill if they eat it. Very quickly, the coyotes avoid the sheep entirely. In this scenario, what are the UCS, CS, and CR, respectively?

(A) The substance, the sheep's wool, aversion to sheep

(B) The sheep's wool, the substance, aversion to sheep

(C) Aversion to sheep, the substance, the sheep's wool

(D) The coyotes, the sheep's wool, aversion to sheep

(E) The substance, the sheep's wool, the coyotes

145. The same ranchers discover that now not only will the coyotes not attack the treated sheep but also they will not attack nearby sheep. This is an example of:

(A) Extinction

(B) Discrimination

(C) Generalization

(D) Spontaneous recovery

(E) Chaining

146. In operant conditioning, the Premack Principle states that:

(A) Punishment is ineffective.

(B) Primary reinforcers are used to reinforce desirable behavior.

(C) Punishment is effective when paired with an aversive stimulus.

(D) Acquiring a desired behavior from an individual can be effectively used as a reinforcer for another, less desirable activity.

(E) More desirable behavior can be achieved through positive reinforcement.

147. Mrs. Jackson, an English teacher, gives pop quizzes to her students every marking period. This is an example of:

(A) Variable interval schedule of reinforcement
(B) Variable ratio schedule of reinforcement
(C) Fixed ratio schedule of reinforcement
(D) Fixed interval schedule of reinforcement
(E) Interval ratio schedule of reinforcement

148. In what manner would Ivan Pavlov have conducted extinction trials on his classically conditioned dogs?

(A) Reinforcing the behavior he wished to extinguish
(B) Repeatedly presenting the conditioned stimulus (bell) without pairing it with the unconditioned stimulus (food)
(C) Repeatedly presenting dogs with the food and the bell at the same time
(D) Immediately giving the dogs food (UCS) after the bell (CS) rings
(E) Repeatedly bringing in different types of food (UCS) and then reinforcing the salivating immediately after

149. In John Watson's "Little Albert" experiment, what was the UCS?

(A) The white rat
(B) The little boy
(C) Anything white and furry
(D) The loud noise
(E) Fear

150. Which of the following is true of classical conditioning?

(A) UCS produces the UCR.
(B) CR produces the CS.
(C) UCR produces the CS.
(D) CS produces the UCS.
(E) UCR produces the UCS.

151. Dylan's mother buys him a sailor's cap before they go on a family fishing trip. On the boat, Dylan gets nauseated and vomits. The next day he gets nauseated just from looking at the sailor's cap. The sailor's cap has become:

(A) The unconditioned stimulus
(B) The conditioned stimulus
(C) The conditioned response
(D) The unconditioned response
(E) The reconditioned stimulus

152. Before Dylan became nauseated, he was able to go fishing with his family, even catching several fish. Fishing is an example of what schedule of reinforcement?

(A) Fixed ratio
(B) Fixed interval
(C) Unfixed interval
(D) Variable ratio
(E) Variable interval

153. Sean sells shoes for a living. His salary depends on how many shoes he can sell in a two-week period of time. What schedule of reinforcement is Sean being paid with?

(A) Variable ratio
(B) Variable interval
(C) Fixed ratio
(D) Fixed interval
(E) None of the above

154. A passenger on an airplane was feeling very anxious about an important job interview the next morning, and as a result he was uneasy and nervous the entire flight. Back home a week later, he is contemplating a holiday trip. Though he hadn't previously been afraid to fly, he finds himself suddenly nervous about flying and decides to cancel his plans to visit an out-of-state relative. What are the UCS, UCR, CS, and CR, respectively?

(A) Job interview, feeling nervous and anxious, flying, feeling nervous and anxious about flying

(B) Feeling nervous and anxious, flying, out-of-state relative, feeling anxious and nervous about flying

(C) Flying, feeling nervous and anxious, job interview, feeling nervous and anxious

(D) Feeling nervous and anxious, job interview, flying, feeling nervous and anxious

(E) Job interview, feeling nervous and anxious, out-of-state relative, feeling nervous and anxious

155. As part of a new and intriguing line of research in behavioral medicine, researchers gave mice saccharine-flavored water and followed it up with an injection of a drug that weakens mice's immune systems. Later, when these mice drank saccharine-flavored water, they showed signs of weakened immune response. Research is currently under way to see if the reverse is possible (if conditioning can be used to increase immune functioning), a discovery that would surely have important implications for new medical treatments. In the initial experiment, what is the saccharine-flavored water?

(A) Unconditioned stimulus

(B) Conditioned stimulus

(C) Conditioned response

(D) Unconditioned response

(E) Stimulus response

156. Advertisements created to attract children, especially those for food products, often feature cartoon characters. Smart advertisers know (and research confirms) that children find advertisements with cartoon characters more persuasive than similar advertisements that do not include a cartoon character. In this scenario, what is the unconditioned response?

(A) The food product
(B) The advertisement
(C) The cartoon character
(D) Desire to buy the food product
(E) Finding the cartoon character fun and relatable

157. In the preceding scenario, in terms of classical conditioning, what is the cartoon character?

(A) The conditioned stimulus
(B) The unconditioned stimulus
(C) The conditioned response
(D) The unconditioned response
(E) The stimulus response

158. Which of the following statements best defines classical conditioning?

(A) A type of learning in which behaviors are produced based on rewards and punishments
(B) A type of learning based on modeling or imitating the behavior of others
(C) A type of learning in which a response naturally elicited by a stimulus comes to be elicited by a formerly neutral stimulus
(D) The process by which experience or practice results in a change in behavior
(E) The process by which voluntary behaviors are produced in the presence of certain stimuli

159. During the conditioning process of Pavlov's dogs, what element of classical conditioning did the bell and food play?

(A) CS and UCS
(B) US and CS
(C) UCS and CS
(D) CS and UCR
(E) CS and CR

160. Desensitization therapy can best be defined as:

(A) A conditioning technique that creates an avoidance of certain foods

(B) A conditioning technique that creates a conditioned response from a formerly neutral stimuli

(C) A conditioning technique that gradually increases one's desire to perform a particular behavior

(D) A conditioning technique that uses generalization to get people to overcome their fears

(E) A conditioning technique designed to gradually reduce anxiety about a particular object or situation

161. Classical conditioning would best be suited to answer which of the following questions?

(A) Why do people repeat behaviors when they are followed by something good?

(B) Why do children know a lot about driving a car before their first time behind the wheel?

(C) Why do people associate certain foods with nausea?

(D) Why are some animals difficult to train to perform certain kinds of behaviors?

(E) Why do people imitate behaviors they see someone else get punished for?

162. Of the following, which would a psychologist consider the best example of learning?

(A) A young man's beard beginning to grow at age 15

(B) A woman experiencing labor pains

(C) Salmon swimming upstream during the mating season

(D) A child being able to ride a bike

(E) A baby sucking on her mother's breast for nourishment

163. The sight of a needle can trigger fear in some people. Why is this an example of classical conditioning?

(A) People learn this when they are young.

(B) There is an unconditioned association with fear and the needle.

(C) Needles hurt.

(D) With positive reinforcement one can overcome their fear.

(E) As people get older they overcome this fear.

CHAPTER 9

Operant Conditioning and Cognitive Learning

164. Mary gives her two young sons a sticker every time they clean up their rooms, take the dog out for a walk, and empty the garbage. When they earn 30 stickers, they can go to the movies. This approach to behavior modification is known as:

(A) A token economy
(B) Positive reinforcement
(C) Primary reinforcement
(D) Cognitive behavioral therapy
(E) Cueing principle

165. The key difference between primary and secondary reinforcement is:

(A) One is a positive form of reinforcement and the other is a negative form of reinforcement.
(B) One is naturally satisfying and unlearned while the other is something learned through positive experience.
(C) One is a form of escape conditioning while the other is a form of avoidance conditioning.
(D) One uses a variable schedule of reinforcement and the other a continuous schedule of reinforcement.
(E) One is an example of operant conditioning and the other of classical conditioning.

166. What is one major difference between operant conditioning and classical conditioning?

(A) Operant conditioning takes place as a result of some voluntary action, while classical conditioning takes place without choice.

(B) Operant conditioning takes place before the response, while classical conditioning takes place after the response.

(C) Operant conditioning is learned by association, while classical conditioning is learned by reinforcement.

(D) Classical conditioning is part of social cognitive learning, while operant conditioning is not.

(E) Classical conditioning has a stimulus but no response, while operant conditioning has both a stimulus and a response.

167. Suspending a basketball player for committing a flagrant foul is an example of:

(A) Negative reinforcement

(B) Positive reinforcement

(C) Punishment

(D) Primary reinforcement

(E) Secondary reinforcement

168. Which of the following statements best explains E. L. Thorndike's law of effect?

(A) Behaviors that are negatively reinforced are more likely to be discontinued than behaviors that are punished.

(B) Receiving reinforcement every time a person performs a good deed, or continuous reinforcement, will increase the likelihood that the person will continue that behavior.

(C) The stimuli of food, water, and sex are innately satisfying and require no learning.

(D) Behaviors are strengthened by positive consequences and weakened by negative ones.

(E) Behaviors are reinforced through primary reinforcers.

169. Davey is a young boy who interacts with the family dog by hugging her. Every time the parents witness this interaction, they take Davey's hand and perform a stroking motion on the dog, followed by praising Davey for being good with the dog and then doing an enjoyable activity with Davey. This procedure is known as:

(A) Reinforcement
(B) Chaining
(C) Primary reinforcers
(D) Secondary reinforcers
(E) Shaping

170. Schedules of reinforcement have a direct effect on maintaining your behavior. Which schedule of reinforcement is represented by your checking of social media to see if your post has received more "likes"?

(A) Fixed interval
(B) Variable interval
(C) Fixed ratio
(D) Variable ratio
(E) Fixed variable

171. What is the goal of both positive and negative reinforcement?

(A) To decrease the likelihood that a negative reinforcer will follow a behavior
(B) To increase the likelihood that the preceding behavior will be repeated
(C) To decrease the likelihood that the preceding behavior will be repeated
(D) To ensure there are no negative consequences following the behavior
(E) To add a primary reinforcer after someone does a proper behavior

172. Latent learning can best be described as:

(A) Learning that depends on the mental process

(B) Learning that is not immediately reflected in a behavior change

(C) A learning technique that provides precise information about one's inner bodily functions

(D) Learning that is based on rewards and punishments

(E) A type of learning that occurs after the behavior has already been done

173. Thorndike's law of effect neglects the inner drives or motives that make learners pursue the "satisfying state," allowing learners to reach their goals. Which of the following psychologists would have agreed with that statement?

(A) Kohler

(B) Pavlov

(C) Tolman

(D) Skinner

(E) Watson

174. Which of the following scenarios is the best example of a cognitive map?

(A) A dog sits by the window an hour before her owner should return home.

(B) A little girl remembers to get her jacket before leaving for school.

(C) A boy follows his big sister home on his bicycle.

(D) When asked for directions to his job, a man recites them in great detail.

(E) A teacher remembers all the names of her students.

175. A chimpanzee is in a cage with a banana on the ground just out of his reach outside of the cage. After a period of inaction, the chimp suddenly grabs the stick in the cage, pokes it through the cage, and drags the banana within reach. This type of learning is called:

(A) Insight

(B) Latent

(C) Cognitive

(D) Operant

(E) Observational

176. Harry Harlow's goal was to get his monkeys to figure out that in any set of six trials, the food was always under the same box. Initially the monkeys chose the boxes randomly, sometimes finding food and sometimes not. However, after a while their behavior changed: after two consistent trials of finding the correct box, they continually went back to the same box. Harlow concluded that the monkeys had "learned how to learn." According to Harlow the monkeys established:

(A) Cognitive maps
(B) Reinforcers
(C) Cognitive sets
(D) Learned maps
(E) Learning sets

177. Which of the following statements best exemplifies the idea behind social cognitive learning?

(A) Learning occurs when we see someone else being punished for a behavior.
(B) Learning is likely to happen whether we see someone else punished or rewarded for behavior.
(C) Learning occurs when we see someone else being rewarded for a behavior.
(D) Learning is simply based on observation.
(E) Learning is based on external rewards and behaviors.

178. In Albert Bandura's "bobo" doll experiment, which group of children spontaneously acted aggressively toward the doll rather quickly?

(A) Model-reward condition
(B) Model-punished condition
(C) No-consequences condition
(D) Reward and punishment condition
(E) No condition

179. Devyn watches a violent television show and then pretends to shoot her brother Tyler with a toy pistol. A psychologist would say that Devyn has learned this behavior through:

(A) Operant conditioning
(B) Classical conditioning
(C) Observational learning
(D) Latent learning
(E) Learning set

180. While taking his math placement exam, Spencer became stuck on one problem. With only five minutes left, he suddenly arrived at the answer. This is an example of:

(A) Latent learning
(B) Insight
(C) Learning set
(D) Abstract learning
(E) Operant conditioning

181. After several attempts at escape with no success, the electrically shocked dogs give up. At that moment the gates open and the dogs could simply walk out, but they don't; instead they just sit there. This could most likely be explained by the concept of:

(A) Latent learning
(B) Spontaneous recovery
(C) Vicarious learning
(D) Learned helplessness
(E) Intrinsic motivation

182. After overcoming her fear of the dentist, Jada finds out she needs a root canal. On her way to the dentist's office, her old fears and anxieties return and she begins to panic. This is an example of:

(A) Generalization
(B) Spontaneous recovery
(C) Discrimination
(D) Insight
(E) Classical conditioning

CHAPTER 10

Memory

183. Katie was able to remember the number 111 by associating it with Admiral Nelson, who happened to have one eye, one arm, and one leg. This is an example of:

(A) Retrieving
(B) Storing
(C) Encoding
(D) Memory
(E) Imagery

184. Which of the following examples best illustrates episodic memory?

(A) Remembering that you got a bicycle for your 12th birthday
(B) Knowing that Christopher Columbus sailed in 1492
(C) Teaching someone how to play tennis
(D) Reciting the alphabet
(E) Understanding a conversation someone is having in a foreign language

185. Sophia's parents taught her how to ride a bike when she was just three years old. Sophia picked up the skill very quickly and has enjoyed riding bikes ever since. When asked how she learned to ride a bike, Sophia is unable to remember the very first time that she successfully rode a bike. This is an example of:

(A) Semantic memory
(B) Episodic memory
(C) Procedural memory
(D) Echoic memory
(E) Iconic memory

186. Clint learned the capitals of all 50 states for a test and can still name them one year later. Which of the following brain structures plays an important role in this type of memory storage?

(A) Thalamus
(B) Hypothalamus
(C) Amygdala
(D) Hippocampus
(E) Cerebrum

187. Suppose you are absorbed in reading a novel and a friend asks you a question. You stop reading and ask, "What did you say?" As soon as the words leave your mouth, you realize you can recall your friend's exact words. What is the reason for your ability to play back these words?

(A) Iconic memory
(B) Echoic memory
(C) Semantic memory
(D) Sensory memory
(E) Short-term memory

188. According to the information-processing model, which is the correct order of inputting information?

(A) Encode semantically, retrieve elaborately, store information
(B) Retrieve from long-term memory, encode in short-term memory, encode in sensory memory
(C) Encode in sensory memory, encode in short-term memory, encode in long-term memory
(D) Store information, retrieve upon demand, encode necessary information
(E) Encode with sensory receptors, store information, retrieve upon demand

189. Which of the following statements is *not* true?

   (A) Deep processing involves elaborate rehearsal.
   (B) Automatic processing is unconscious encoding of information.
   (C) Interference results when new information enters short-term memory and pushes out old information.
   (D) Levels of processing theory says that remembering depends on how information is encoded.
   (E) Declarative memory involves memories for skills, habits, and things learned through classical conditioning.

190. While walking home from a party drunk, Jeff witnessed a crime. When questioned by the police the following day, he could not remember what he saw. After drinking some liquor, Jeff remembered the crime. This phenomenon best illustrates:

   (A) The framing effect
   (B) Short-term memory loss
   (C) Hypnotic amnesia
   (D) State-dependent memory
   (E) Anterograde amnesia

191. Which type of memory is also referred to as working memory?

   (A) Long-term memory
   (B) Short-term memory
   (C) Sensory memory
   (D) Semantic memory
   (E) Episodic memory

192. The ability to maintain exact detailed visual memories over a significant period of time is called:

   (A) Flashbulb memory
   (B) Semantic memory
   (C) Eidetic memory
   (D) Echoic memory
   (E) Iconic memory

193. If a rat has its amygdala destroyed, which of the following types of memories is it likely to lose?

(A) Emotional
(B) Procedural
(C) Factual
(D) Iconic
(E) Visual

194. The primacy effect is best explained by which of the following statements?

(A) Items on a list with unique meaning are more likely to be remembered.
(B) The first items on a list are likely to be more effectively rehearsed and therefore more likely to be remembered.
(C) Items on a list presented more recently are more likely to be remembered.
(D) Items on a list with simplistic meaning are more likely to be remembered.
(E) The last items on a list are more likely to be encoded first and therefore remembered.

195. During his English class, Ben is able to recall the author of *The Scarlet Letter*. This type of memory is called:

(A) Procedural
(B) Episodic
(C) Long term
(D) Semantic
(E) Constructive

196. Which of the following statements best explains one major difference between short-term memory and long-term memory?

(A) Long-term memory is unlimited in capacity while short-term memory is not.

(B) Long-term memory holds only episodic memories while short-term memory does not.

(C) Long-term memory varies a great deal from one person to another, while short-term memory does not.

(D) In terms of processing, long-term memory comes directly after sensory memory while short-term memory does not.

(E) Long-term memory depends on neural connections in the limbic system while short-term memory does not.

197. Maintenance rehearsal involves:

(A) Recalling the words at the end of a list

(B) Intentionally repeating information

(C) Processing visual memories

(D) Systematically recalling information

(E) Processing iconic memories

198. During a job interview, a manager introduces Linda to the company's staff of 20 people while showing her around the office. Linda tries to remember their names during the introductions but almost immediately forgets all their names once the interview with the manager resumes. This is an example of which memory process?

(A) Short-term memory

(B) Sensory memory

(C) Automatic processing

(D) Echoic memory

(E) Iconic memory

199. After forgetting the combination to several other locks, Nate was trying to find a way to remember the combination to the new lock he bought last week. The combination is 19, 20, 9. To remember the combination, he thinks of the year 1929. His method to remember this is an example of:

(A) Elaborate rehearsal
(B) Maintenance rehearsal
(C) Short-term memory
(D) Chunking
(E) Decoding

200. The process of encoding information from short-term memory to long-term memory is most efficient when it:

(A) Has a procedural manner
(B) Involves some kind of association
(C) Uses repetition
(D) Does not use repetition
(E) Uses semantic memory

201. Maintenance rehearsal is to elaborate rehearsal as:

(A) Long-term memory is to short-term memory
(B) Sensory memory is to long-term memory
(C) Short-term memory is to long-term memory
(D) Sensory memory is to short-term memory
(E) Automatic memory is to long-term memory

202. Which of the following is *not* an example of effortful encoding?

(A) Maintenance rehearsal
(B) Repetition
(C) Meaningful associations
(D) Chunking
(E) Transferring information from STM to LTM

CHAPTER 11

Remembering and Forgetting

203. Which of the following statements is correct regarding why eyewitness testimony is *not* always accurate?

(A) People do not have the capacity to remember.
(B) People may be asked misleading questions.
(C) People do not have a strong recognition.
(D) People do not have a strong ability to recall past information.
(E) People lie too often.

204. What is the correct name of the memory files that contain related information about a specific topic or category?

(A) Prototypes
(B) Nerve cells
(C) Nodes
(D) Networks
(E) Schemas

205. One of the earliest psychologists to study memory and forgetting was Hermann Ebbinghaus, who tested his own recall of a list of nonsense syllables, previously learned through rehearsal. He then came up with the concept of a forgetting curve. This suggests:

(A) Remembering nonsense syllables can be encoded faster than meaningful information.
(B) Old information will interfere with new information being encoded into LTM.
(C) New information will interfere with old information already stored in LTM.
(D) Recall of meaningless information drops soon after initial learning and then levels off.
(E) Recall of meaningless information cannot be retrieved more than three hours after encoding.

206. Maya is currently enrolled in an Italian class at her local college. While on spring break, Maya travels to Italy. She is excited to practice her new skills, but when she gets there she is having trouble. Every time she tries to speak Italian, Spanish words she learned in high school come out. This is an example of:

(A) Retroactive interference
(B) Proactive interference
(C) Retrograde amnesia
(D) Anterograde amnesia
(E) Dissociative interference

207. Sydney sustained a head injury while playing a hockey game and had to be taken to the hospital. When questioned by the doctor, Sydney could not remember anything about the game or the entire day before the game. This is an example of:

(A) Psychogenic amnesia
(B) Anterograde amnesia
(C) Retrograde amnesia
(D) Global amnesia
(E) Long-term memory amnesia

208. Jayden consciously pushes the due date for his term project out of his mind, so much so that on the day it is due, Jayden must take an incomplete from his teacher. This is an example of:

(A) Repression
(B) Aggression
(C) Amnesia
(D) Forgetting
(E) Suppression

209. After his car accident, Paul cannot make any new memories. In fact, to remember his daily activities Paul must write everything down. This is known as:

(A) Retrograde amnesia
(B) Anterograde amnesia
(C) Proactive interference
(D) Retroactive interference
(E) Dissociative amnesia

210. The method of loci includes which of the following three steps?

(A) Create visual places, memorize those places, create vivid imagery

(B) Create vivid associations, memorize visual sequences, put associations into places

(C) Memorize visual sequence of places, create vivid associations, put associations into selected places

(D) Memorize selected places, create vivid imagery, memorize vivid imagery

(E) Create vivid associations, memorize associations, put associations into places

211. Michael was hit by a car while riding his bicycle and suffered a severe brain injury. Afterwards, Michael was still able to ride his bicycle but could no longer remember that his mother taught him how to ride. Which part of Michael's brain was most likely affected by the accident?

(A) Hypothalamus

(B) Thalamus

(C) Amygdala

(D) Hippocampus

(E) Medulla

212. To study how we forget encoded memories, Hermann Ebbinghaus learned lists of nonsense syllables and then recorded how well he retained the lists up to 30 days later. He found that memory for new information undergoes an initially rapid drop-off but then levels out after several days. This result is known as:

(A) Proactive interference

(B) Retroactive interference

(C) The forgetting curve

(D) Encoding failure

(E) Episodic interference

213. Which of the following exemplifies retrograde interference?

(A) Ella failed her French test because she was confusing it with Spanish words she studied last year.

(B) Ava, a medical student, failed her test on the bones in the hand because she studied for the bones in the foot after studying the hand.

(C) Isabella can no longer form new memories after her head trauma.

(D) Nya remembers only the last three items her mom put on the grocery shopping list.

(E) Emma cannot remember her third-grade teacher's name, but she does remember her fourth-grade teacher's name.

214. After studying for a test, Jack realized he remembered exactly where a particular piece of information appeared on a page in his textbook, even though he did not try to remember the item. This is an example of:

(A) Explicit memory

(B) Procedural memory

(C) Declarative memory

(D) Implicit memory

(E) Semantic memory

215. A child recognizes a dog the first time he sees one in real life after having seen pictures of dogs. This involves which of the following?

(A) Retrieving previously learned information without the presence of any cues

(B) Using the available cues to identify information that has already been learned

(C) Filling in a specific amount of information without the use of any newly learned cues

(D) Using available cues to create an entirely new response

(E) Encoding new information to replace previously learned information

216. Corey sits at his kitchen table to think about what he needs to buy at the grocery store. He is using his ability to:

(A) Recognize
(B) Recite
(C) Memorize
(D) Recall
(E) Initiate

217. After making a mess of the playroom, Mason visualizes where each toy should be placed in the room. He is using:

(A) Method of loci
(B) Peg method
(C) Visualization
(D) Elaborate rehearsal
(E) Procedural memory

218. Based on Hermann Ebbinghaus's forgetting curve research using nonsense syllables, unfamiliar information is:

(A) Forgotten within the first eight hours
(B) Forgotten within the first hour
(C) Forgotten within the first day
(D) Forgotten within the first two days
(E) Forgotten within the first week

219. The forgetting curve measures which of the following?

(A) The amount of previously learned information that subjects remember across time
(B) The amount of new information that can remain in the short-term memory
(C) Memory that cannot be consciously remembered over time
(D) The amount of information children can retain over age five
(E) The amount of information one can memorize in any given day

220. Recognition is to recall as:

(A) Fill-in is to multiple choice
(B) Fill-in is to essay
(C) Multiple choice is to fill-in
(D) Multiple choice is to essay
(E) Multiple choice is to matching

221. Kimberly knows she did something embarrassing at her friend's birthday party many years before, but she cannot remember what it was. This is an example of:

(A) Repression
(B) Amnesia
(C) Forgetting curve
(D) Implicit memory
(E) Interference

CHAPTER 12

Intelligence and Testing

222. IQ tests for military draftees in NATO countries in Europe have confirmed a trend of rising scores over time. This is an example of which of the following?

(A) Cultural malleability of intelligence
(B) Piaget's theory of intelligence
(C) Vygotsky's theory of intelligence
(D) Law of individual differences
(E) The Flynn effect

223. A psychologist has developed a new test of intelligence. When compared with an established intelligence test, the new test gave the same IQ values (within measurement error). As a result, the new test is considered to be:

(A) Reliable
(B) Valid
(C) Accurate
(D) Standardized
(E) Comparative

224. Two parents would like to have their child attend a prestigious preschool. To gain admittance, their child must take a test that evaluates her potential to learn in the hopes of predicting future performance. This type of test is called:

(A) An IQ test
(B) An achievement test
(C) An intelligence test
(D) An aptitude test
(E) An ability test

225. If a four-year-old girl correctly answered questions on an intelligence exam similar to a five-year-old girl, she would be said to have a mental age of five. In this case her intelligence quotient (IQ) would be:

(A) 100
(B) 95
(C) 150
(D) 125
(E) 110

226. Which of the following psychologists added a performance scale in an attempt to measure nonverbal skills and rule out other cultural or educational biases?

(A) Wechsler
(B) Binet
(C) Gardner
(D) Sternberg
(E) Terman

227. Charles Spearman's two-factor theory of intelligence referred to which of the following?

(A) Mathematical skills and spatial intelligence
(B) Analytical problem-solving and interpersonal skills
(C) Ability to perform complex mental work and mathematical or verbal skills
(D) Analytical problem-solving and intrapersonal skills
(E) Ability to reason logically and demonstrate written language and thinking skills

228. Robert Sternberg's triarchic theory of intelligence was divided into three categories. Which three categories are correct?

(A) Practical, intrapersonal, creative
(B) Experimental, analytical, problem solving
(C) Experimental, problem solving, practical
(D) Analytical, logical, practical
(E) Analytical, creative, practical

229. According to Raymond Cattell, what is the major difference between crystallized intelligence and fluid intelligence?

(A) Crystallized intelligence refers to problem-solving abilities, while fluid intelligence is the ability to absorb and retain information.

(B) Crystallized intelligence is the ability to absorb and retain information, while fluid intelligence refers to problem-solving abilities.

(C) Crystallized intelligence is the ability to be analytical, while fluid intelligence is the ability to read and write.

(D) Crystallized intelligence is the ability to read and write, while fluid intelligence is the ability to be analytical.

(E) Crystallized intelligence is the ability to absorb information, while fluid intelligence is the ability to analyze the information.

230. Which of the following types of tests measures the capacity of a test-taker to perform some task or role in the future?

(A) Achievement

(B) Aptitude

(C) Conventional

(D) Self-monitored

(E) Adult intelligence scale

231. A savant can best be defined as:

(A) A mentally handicapped individual

(B) A child between the ages of 8 and 12 who suffers from autism

(C) A mentally handicapped individual with exceptional ability in mathematical calculations, memory, art, or music

(D) A male adult who suffers from delusional thoughts and erratic behavior

(E) A social loner who has exceptional abilities in the field of science or math

232. Which of the following psychologists did *not* suggest the existence of more than one kind of intelligence?

(A) Gardner

(B) Sternberg

(C) Guilford

(D) Thurstone

(E) Spearman

233. The American Psychiatric Association established IQ ranges for various levels of intellectual disability. Below 25 is considered to be:

(A) Profound intellectual disability
(B) Severe intellectual disability
(C) Mild intellectual disability
(D) Moderate intellectual disability
(E) Extreme intellectual disability

234. The WAIS and the WISC are credited for:

(A) Creating early intervention programs for the mentally ill
(B) Creating intelligence tests specific to different age groups
(C) Creating one standardized test equal for all cultures and races
(D) Creating a new understanding of the term *mental age*
(E) Creating intelligence tests that only test verbal skills

235. The MMPI (Minnesota multiphasic inventories) is designed to:

(A) Measure a person's verbal and mathematical skills
(B) Measure a student's academic potential
(C) Require students to tell stories about a particular photograph
(D) Identify characteristics of personality and behavior
(E) Measure the aptitude of high school students

236. Alfred Binet is known as the father of intelligence mainly because of his work in:

(A) The assessment of one's ability to learn and the creation of the mental age
(B) The creation of the intelligence quotient (IQ)
(C) The creation of both the mental age and the intelligence quotient
(D) The assessment of one's ability to learn and the intelligence quotient
(E) The understanding of the heritability factors in terms of intelligence

237. Because Lela did not want to raise her child in poverty, she put her baby up for adoption. A middle-class family, in a good home, is now raising Lela's baby. What effect could this have on the child's IQ?

(A) It will probably be lower than the IQs of children who stay with their biological parents.

(B) It will not be significantly different from the IQs of children who stay in a disadvantaged setting.

(C) It will be higher than the IQs of children who stay in disadvantaged settings only if the adoptive parents have above-average IQs.

(D) It may be as much as 10 to 15 points higher than the IQs of children who stay in disadvantaged settings.

(E) It will make no difference because an individual's IQ is based solely on genetic factors.

238. The concept of reaction range indicates that:

(A) Intelligence is fixed at birth because it is based on genetic factors.

(B) Intelligence may increase or decrease as a result of the environment.

(C) Intelligence is completely variable due to environmental factors.

(D) Heredity establishes a very narrow range for intellectual development.

(E) Intelligence is completely determined by age five.

239. If genetic factors contribute to IQ scores, then fraternal twins should have:

(A) Less similar IQ scores than identical twins

(B) More similar IQ scores than identical twins

(C) IQ scores more similar than those of siblings

(D) Completely different IQ scores

(E) No connection at all

240. Which of following pairs are likely to have the strongest negative correlation for intelligence?

(A) Fraternal twins raised apart

(B) Unrelated children raised together

(C) Adopted children and their adoptive parents

(D) Adopted children and their birth parents

(E) Identical twins raised apart

241. Robert Sternberg believed people possessed multiple intelligences and proposed a theory of three intelligences. According to Sternberg, the three intelligences were:

(A) Interpersonal intelligence, mathematical intelligence, and spatial intelligence
(B) Emotional intelligence, analytical intelligence, and bodily kinesthetic intelligence
(C) Logical intelligence, emotional intelligence, and spatial intelligence
(D) Analytical intelligence, creative intelligence, and practical intelligence
(E) Emotional intelligence, creative intelligence, and bodily kinesthetic intelligence

CHAPTER 13

Thought and Language

242. Because it has all the features commonly associated with the concept of a dog, a poodle is considered:

(A) An algorithm
(B) A heuristic
(C) A prototype
(D) A phoneme
(E) A concept

243. Which of the following is an example of functional fixedness?

(A) Using a blanket as a floor mat
(B) Not being able to solve a math problem because you are using the incorrect formula
(C) Replacing oil with applesauce when baking a cake
(D) Failing to use your keys to open a package when you can't find a pair of scissors
(E) Picking up a tangerine and calling it an orange

244. To become a chess or checkers champion one must use:

(A) Algorithms
(B) Heuristics
(C) Concepts
(D) Prototypes
(E) Morphemes

245. After watching the evening news, Khloe believes the newscast contains only tragic events like floods, earthquakes, and murders. When asked to think carefully about the newscast, she did recall many other events. This is an example of:

(A) Representative heuristic
(B) Availability heuristic
(C) Algorithm
(D) Functional fixedness
(E) Insight

246. Compared to divergent thinkers, convergent thinkers are more likely to:

(A) Think "outside the box" when problem solving
(B) Generate many different solutions when problem solving
(C) Choose to problem solve using an algorithm rather than a heuristic
(D) Use representative heuristics to problem solve
(E) Never allow functional fixedness to get in the way of problem solving

247. On her way to London, Janet was invited into the cockpit to meet the pilot, Alex. She was surprised to see that Alex was a woman. This is an example of:

(A) Confirmation bias
(B) Convergent thinking
(C) Insight
(D) Representative heuristic
(E) Availability heuristic

248. Phonemes are best defined as:

(A) The smallest meaningful combination of sounds in a language
(B) The basic sounds of consonants and vowels
(C) Something that specifies the meanings of words and phrases
(D) A set of rules that specify how we combine words to form meaningful sentences
(E) A special form of communication

249. Noam Chomsky's language theory includes the idea that:

(A) Language development occurs between the ages of three and five.

(B) Children learn language through positive and negative reinforcement.

(C) Children make the same grammatical errors as their parents.

(D) Children model language development from those around them.

(E) Children have an innate mental grammar.

250. A cognitive framework that helps organize and interpret information is called:

(A) Associative learning

(B) A schema

(C) Observational learning

(D) Mirroring

(E) Modeling

251. Which of the following statements is *not* supported by the Sapir-Whorf linguistic relativity hypothesis?

(A) The language a person speaks determines the way a person thinks.

(B) If language lacks expression, the thought that corresponds will likely not occur.

(C) There is evidence to support that language development has inborn tendencies.

(D) If language affects our ability to store information, it should affect our thought process.

(E) To understand new vocabulary, it is easier to think about the relationship between language and thought.

252. Suppose you consider elderly people to be infirm and mentally slow. Every time you see elderly people in need of care or assistance, you take it as evidence of your belief, while ignoring the many cases of healthy, active elderly people. This is an example of:

(A) Representative heuristic

(B) Availability heuristic

(C) Prototype

(D) Confirmation bias

(E) Functional fixedness

253. Annie is having a conflict with her friend. When faced with this stressful situation, Annie does not directly address her friend to resolve the conflict. Instead, she avoids her friend and shifts her focus toward helping herself deal with the feeling of stress. Which of the following best describe Annie's strategy?

(A) Problem-focused coping
(B) Emotion-focused coping
(C) Learned helplessness
(D) Internal locus of control
(E) External locus of control

254. Which of the following sentences best explains the idea of overregularization?

(A) Yesterday I goed to the store.
(B) I ain't going to the store.
(C) I no want to go to store.
(D) I want store.
(E) No store please.

255. Which of the following psychologists believes in the LAD, the language acquisition device?

(A) Whorf
(B) Seligman
(C) Kahneman
(D) Chomsky
(E) Sapir

256. When Michelle's father tells her that Mama is coming home, Michelle says only one word in reply, "Mama," and repeats this one word when her father asks if she wants to play with Mama when she gets home. This is an example of:

(A) Telegraphic speech
(B) Syntax
(C) Morpheme
(D) The one-word stage
(E) Phoneme

257. Which of the following statements best illustrates the concept of framing?

(A) A PSA for breast mammograms chooses to use the statement "you can die if you don't," rather than "this can save your life."

(B) Lily assumes her doctor named Chris is a male, when in fact she is female.

(C) An advertiser uses divergent thinking to come up with a commercial slogan.

(D) A person remembers items on a list depending on which order they appear in.

(E) A cigarette company puts beautiful women in its commercials.

258. Which of the following terms is an example of an innate sound program in the brain that involves making and processing sounds that will eventually be used to form words?

(A) Grammar
(B) Babbling
(C) Talking
(D) Sentences
(E) Morphemes

259. Rules of grammar can best be defined as:

(A) Acquiring language through four stages
(B) Phonemes and morphemes
(C) Problem solving using language
(D) Forming sentences that range from three to eight words
(E) Speaking in sentences that are stated in different ways but have the same meaning

260. Two-year-old Tina enjoys books with pictures of horses. When she visits a farm, she sees a cow and calls him a horse because he is large and has long legs, big ears, and a tail. However, her mother tells her the animal is actually a cow and then takes her to see a real horse. With this new information, Tina is able to update her concept of a horse and add a new concept for a cow. This is an example of which of the following?

(A) Confirmation bias
(B) Heuristic
(C) Intuition
(D) Framing
(E) A schema

261. Which of the following statements best describes an example of availability heuristic?

(A) After speaking in front of 200 people, Tim is no longer afraid of public speaking.

(B) Jane thinks all men will eventually cheat on her.

(C) Steven knows a lot of smart students at his high school and believes students from his school are smarter than students at another nearby high school, even though the other school won a debate contest with Steven's school.

(D) Rob claims that when he is confronted with a problem, he likes to come up with one correct solution.

(E) After playing the same slot machine for an hour, Todd refuses to go to another machine, believing his luck is about to change.

262. Which of the following statements best defines information retrieval?

(A) Having memories of your 16th birthday party

(B) Thinking all dog owners are sensitive people

(C) Memorizing information that might be needed in an emergency

(D) Picking out the proper outfit to wear to a friend's housewarming party

(E) Writing a term paper

263. When solving an anagram one must try every possible combination of letters until the hidden word appears. This is an example of:

(A) A heuristic

(B) A concept

(C) A subgoal

(D) An image

(E) An algorithm

264. Which of the following terms is *not* an example of a problem-solving technique?

(A) Functional fixedness

(B) Trial and error

(C) Subgoals

(D) Brainstorming

(E) Heuristics

265. This problem-solving technique involves analyzing the difference between the current situation and the desired end, and then doing something to reduce that difference.

(A) Subgoals
(B) Means-end analysis
(C) Brainstorming
(D) Heuristic
(E) Algorithm

CHAPTER 14

Motivation

266. William Masters and Virginia Johnson developed the sexual response cycle. Which of the following is *not* a part of the cycle?

(A) Excitement
(B) Plateau
(C) Orgasm
(D) Transcendence
(E) Resolution

267. Motivation can best be defined as:

(A) An innate biological force that produces a fixed set of behaviors
(B) Various physiological and psychological factors that cause a person to act in a particular way
(C) A biological state in which an organism lacks something essential for survival
(D) The tendency or need for a body to stay in a balanced state
(E) Environmental factors that reward, reinforce, or encourage our behavior

268. Repulsion, curiosity, pugnacity, and humility are all examples of:

(A) Needs
(B) Emotions
(C) Instincts
(D) Motivations
(E) Incentives

269. If a person does not eat for a period of time, it causes a need for food. This need produces a state of tension. The tension energizes the person to act in some way to find food, thereby returning the body to homeostasis. This is an example of:

(A) Intrinsic action pattern

(B) Sympathetic nervous system

(C) Extrinsic motivation

(D) Drive reduction theory

(E) Biological needs

270. A fixed action pattern is best illustrated by which of the following examples?

(A) Jackie's need to climb mountains

(B) Marlon's motivation to make a lot of money

(C) A baboon rising on his hind feet when threatened

(D) A dog sitting by the window an hour before his owner comes home

(E) Michael's cat purring when she hears the can opener

271. Which of the following examples best illustrates an intrinsic motivation?

(A) Running a marathon to support breast cancer

(B) Rock climbing to win first prize

(C) Graduating with honors

(D) Trying out for the high school basketball team

(E) A teacher praising a student when she raises her hand

272. Which of the following statements best illustrates Maslow's love and belonging needs?

(A) Getting a raise that helps you pay all of your bills more easily

(B) Moving out of your parents' home for the first time

(C) Beginning to form your first serious romantic relationship

(D) Landing a dream job in your career field

(E) Publishing your memoir

273. Which of the following statements best illustrates Maslow's need for self-actualization?

(A) Obtaining health insurance from your employer

(B) Getting a full eight hours of sleep after staying up with your sick child two nights in a row

(C) Receiving a top score on a university exam

(D) Attending church every week

(E) Quitting your job and moving to Africa to do philanthropic work

274. Which of the following statements best illustrates Maslow's esteem needs?

(A) Moving to a safe community to raise your children

(B) Going to school to earn a master's degree in counseling

(C) Getting married to your high school sweetheart

(D) Donating a large sum of money to charity

(E) Going to the gym three days a week to improve your health

275. Which of the following factors signals hunger in our body?

(A) High levels of glucose

(B) Stimulation of the lateral hypothalamus

(C) Stimulation of the ventromedial hypothalamus

(D) High levels of cholecystokinin

(E) Stomach contractions

276. Homeostasis is best defined as:

(A) The physiological need to satisfy your hunger or thirst

(B) The body's tendency to maintain balance

(C) The arousal of the autonomic nervous system

(D) The release of the hormone serotonin

(E) The biological need for safety and security

277. If the ventromedial hypothalamus of a rat is destroyed:

(A) The rat will starve to death.

(B) The rat will only eat when he feels hungry.

(C) The rat will begin to feel full.

(D) The rat will become obese.

(E) The rat's blood glucose level will remain constant.

278. Which of the following statements best defines set point?

(A) It refers to how efficiently the body breaks food down.

(B) It refers to how quickly the body turns food into energy.

(C) It controls the body's metabolism.

(D) It plays a role in influencing appetite.

(E) It refers to a certain level of body fat that the body maintains.

279. An individual with a low metabolic rate is:

(A) More likely to have a fatter body

(B) Less likely to have a fatter body

(C) Less likely to store excess fuel

(D) More likely to eat more than someone with a high metabolic rate

(E) More likely to have an easier time losing weight

280. Which of the following is *not* an example of a psychological hunger factor?

(A) Social-cultural

(B) Learned associations

(C) Personality traits

(D) Peer pressure

(E) Nutrition

281. An individual's subjective experience and feeling of being either a male or female is referred to as:

(A) Gender roles

(B) Sexual orientation

(C) Gender identity

(D) Transgender

(E) Sex categories

282. By age five, children have acquired many of the complex thoughts and behaviors that accompany being male or female. This is best known as:

(A) Gender identity

(B) Gender roles

(C) Sexual identity

(D) Sexual cognition

(E) Gender cognition

283. Which of the following brain structures is most responsible for hunger and satiety, respectively?

(A) The ventromedial hypothalamus, the lateral hypothalamus
(B) The lateral hypothalamus, the ventromedial hypothalamus
(C) The amygdala, the hippocampus
(D) The hippocampus, the amygdala
(E) The cerebellum, the lateral hypothalamus

284. Which of the following statements is the core concept of Maslow's hierarchy of needs?

(A) Individuals who fail to reach self-actualization feel a sense of failure.
(B) Level 1 is the need for safety and security.
(C) Men are more concerned with safety needs and women are more concerned with esteem needs.
(D) Physiological and other lower-level needs must be reasonably well-satisfied before an individual can become concerned with higher needs such as self-actualization.
(E) An individual can skip levels 1, 2, and 3 and go directly to finding success at level 4.

285. A journalist chooses to go to Afghanistan to cover the war hoping to acquire the admiration of his peers and a promotion. Which of the following theories of motivation best explains this decision?

(A) Drive theory
(B) Incentive theory
(C) Fixed action pattern
(D) Socio-cognitive theory
(E) Motivation

286. Motivation starts with an individual's:

(A) Emotion
(B) Arousal
(C) Need
(D) Drive
(E) Incentive

287. Bill is a manager of 20 employees in a large tire shop. He spurs his workers on with rewards, such as bonuses, or threats of punishment, such as time off without pay. According to American psychologist Douglas McGregor in his book *The Human Side of Enterprise*, Bill is using which theory to motivate workers?

(A) Theory X
(B) Theory Y
(C) Equity theory
(D) Instinct theory
(E) Drive theory

288. Sex researcher Alfred Kinsey developed a continuum known as the Kinsey Scale. This scale states that:

(A) Sexual behavior falls on a continuum ranging from exclusive heterosexuality to exclusive homosexuality.
(B) Women's interest and experience in sex falls on a continuum that is different from males.
(C) Bodily reactions to sexual stimulation can be mapped.
(D) Normal and abnormal sexual activities fall on a continuum.
(E) A series of cultural scenarios are the "cultural narratives" constructed around sexuality.

CHAPTER 15

Emotion

289. Which of the following sequences is correct according to the James-Lange theory of emotion?

(A) Physiological changes, feel emotion, interpretation of emotion, observable behavior

(B) Physiological changes, awareness of physiological change, feel emotion, observable behavior

(C) Feel emotion, physiological changes, interpretation of physiological change, observable behavior

(D) Brain interpretation, physiological changes, observable behavior

(E) Interpretation of stimuli, brain interpretation, physiological changes, observable behavior

290. Jim and June both witnessed the same traffic accident. June witnessed the accident while driving in the opposite direction, while Jim was walking on the sidewalk adjacent to the accident. As a result, Jim and June's physical reactions and perceptions of the same accident were very different, causing different emotional reactions. This is an example of which theory?

(A) Two-factor theory

(B) Spillover effect

(C) Cognitive-appraisal theory

(D) Affective-primacy theory

(E) James-Lange theory

291. What was one major criticism of the James-Lange theory on emotion?

(A) Emotions are usually associated with one specific physiological change in the body.

(B) Physiological changes do not vary in intensity.

(C) Different emotions are not necessarily associated with different patterns of physiological responses.

(D) Most emotions do not need a large amount of interpretation.

(E) Cognition has no direct effect on the physiological changes in the body.

292. Which of the following theories on emotion assumes that our interpretation or appraisal of a situation is the primary cause of emotion?

(A) Cannon-Bard theory

(B) Facial feedback theory

(C) James-Lange theory

(D) Schachter-Singer theory

(E) Peripheral theory

293. Which of the following statements best supports the Schachter-Singer theory of emotion?

(A) A friend walks up to you and tells you he saw someone back into your car and drive away—making you angry.

(B) You hear a loud noise, your heart starts to pound, and you feel scared.

(C) You feel sad because you are crying.

(D) You know you are happy because you have been smiling all day.

(E) Your heart is racing but you are not sure why.

294. Which of the following describes the facial feedback effect?

(A) Facial expressions for basic emotions are universal across cultures.

(B) Different genders tend to exhibit different levels of nonverbal behavior.

(C) We interpret facial expressions in the context of other behaviors and nonverbal cues.

(D) The state of your facial muscles tends to elicit corresponding feelings such as anger or happiness.

(E) Children learn how to exhibit facial expressions by observing their parents.

295. Which of the following statements supports the results of the Ekman-Friesen experiment?

(A) Facial expressions for basic emotions are universal across cultures.

(B) It is difficult to communicate with people of different cultures.

(C) People show disgust for many different reasons.

(D) Babies smile due to modeling behavior.

(E) Children exhibit emotion differently than adults do.

296. Which statement best exemplifies the Yerkes-Dodson law?

(A) Many of Leo's friends think he is depressed due to his lack of any facial expressions.

(B) Josh has a look of disgust on his face after smelling the rotten milk.

(C) Linda spends hours playing a challenging video game because this activity arouses and motivates her.

(D) William's test anxiety helps him score higher on the exam.

(E) Jacob falls asleep in his physics class after being so bored.

297. Happiness includes all of the following except:

(A) Feeling a positive emotion

(B) Being satisfied with your life

(C) Not experiencing a negative emotion

(D) Having a high-paying job

(E) Both environmental and inherited factors

298. Three weeks after winning the lottery, Tanya gave birth to Sophia. Tanya claimed that winning the lottery was the most exciting thing to happen to her until she gave birth to her daughter. This is an example of:

(A) The adaptation-level theory
(B) The rules of happiness theory
(C) The Yerkes-Dodson law
(D) The psychoevolutionary theory
(E) The relative deprivation theory

299. An interpretation or appraisal of a situation as having a positive or negative impact on your life resulting in a subjective feeling is called:

(A) The affective-primacy theory
(B) The James-Lange theory
(C) The Cannon-Bard theory
(D) The facial feedback theory
(E) The cognitive-appraisal theory

300. While sitting in a waiting room, a man next to you begins yelling and acting aggressively. Your heart begins beating fast. You interpret your environmental cues as the cause of your arousal. Which theory of emotion would support this explanation?

(A) The James-Lange theory
(B) The Schachter-Singer theory
(C) The affective-primacy theory
(D) All of the above
(E) None of the above

301. Alice sees a snake and begins to simultaneously feel fear and start trembling. What theory of emotions does this represent?

(A) The James-Lange theory
(B) The Schachter-Singer theory
(C) The Cannon-Bard theory
(D) The cognitive-appraisal theory
(E) The affective-primacy theory

302. When John gets promoted his coworker, Alice, feels resentful, thinking that she was more deserving of the promotion. Which of the following theories of emotion does this instance reflect?

(A) The cognitive-appraisal theory
(B) The Cannon-Bard theory
(C) The facial feedback theory
(D) The James-Lange theory
(E) The peripheral theory

303. "We feel sorry when we cry and afraid because we tremble." This quote is supported by which theory of emotion?

(A) The Cannon-Bard theory
(B) The James-Lange theory
(C) The Cannon-Lange theory
(D) The James-Bard theory
(E) The facial feedback theory

304. Larry really wants to buy his wife the diamond watch she always wanted for her birthday, but he knows he should be more conservative with his money. What type of conflict is he facing?

(A) Approach-approach
(B) Approach-avoidance
(C) Avoidance-avoidance
(D) Positive approach
(E) Negative approach

305. Which of the following examples best illustrates the concept of approach-approach conflict?

(A) Ariel must work at Bloomingdale's while in college.
(B) Sabrina is forced to call the home of one of her students because he is not doing his homework.
(C) Latoya has to choose between Princeton and Yale Universities.
(D) Wendy just got a promotion, but she now has to fire someone else.
(E) Randy works as a stand-up comedian, but he needs to make more money.

306. According to the Cannon-Bard theory of emotion, which part of the brain is vital in terms of physiological responses to emotion?

(A) The cerebellum
(B) The temporal lobe
(C) The frontal lobe
(D) The limbic system
(E) The left hemisphere

307. If we are about to jump out of an airplane for the first time, we tend to feel extreme fear along with low levels of elation. Later, when we decide to jump again, we experience more elation and less fear. This scenario is supported by which theory of emotion?

(A) The James-Lange theory
(B) The affective-primacy theory
(C) The opponent-process theory
(D) The Cannon-Bard theory
(E) None of the above

308. Emotional responses develop before complex thinking occurs. Which of the following psychologists would agree with this statement?

(A) Ekman
(B) Schachter
(C) Bard
(D) Lange
(E) Zajonc

309. Which area of Mary's brain is extremely stimulated when Mary hears a news story that makes her sad?

(A) Hypothalamus
(B) Thalamus
(C) Temporal lobe
(D) Parietal lobe
(E) Amygdala

310. Which example best illustrates the adaptation-level theory?

(A) Michelle takes her mother's inheritance for granted.

(B) Regina has so much to do with so little free time to do it in.

(C) Natasha hired another assistant to help lessen her workload.

(D) Cathryn lost her brand-new wallet and bought a more expensive one.

(E) Alexis sold her engagement ring to send her son to college.

311. To achieve high performance on a simple task, the Yerkes-Dodson law recommends:

(A) High arousal

(B) Low arousal

(C) Medium arousal

(D) Extreme anxiety

(E) Moderate anxiety

CHAPTER 16

Developmental Psychology: Infancy and Childhood

312. Cross-sectional research differs from longitudinal research in that:

(A) Cross-sectional research studies the developmental changes of subjects who are of different ages.

(B) Cross-sectional research studies developmental changes using the same group of subjects over time as they grow older.

(C) Cross-sectional research is more reliable than developmental research.

(D) Cross-sectional research is too specific to the group of people being used for research.

(E) Cross-sectional research takes too much time to gather results.

313. Of the following sets of themes, which pair best represents the core emphasis of developmental psychology?

(A) Cross-sectional versus longitudinal and self-esteem versus self-doubt

(B) Individual versus shared and stability versus change

(C) Young versus old and stability versus change

(D) Individual versus shared and young versus old

(E) Stability versus change and self-esteem versus self-doubt

314. Which of the following is *not* true concerning teratogens?

(A) The impact of a teratogen depends on the genotype of the organism.

(B) Damage from teratogens is always evident at birth.

(C) Impact of teratogens depends on the dosage.

(D) Impact of teratogens often depends on the quality of the postnatal environment.

(E) The impact of teratogens changes the course of perinatal development.

315. Temperament is best defined as:

(A) Personality traits inherited from biological parents that influence emotional reactivity

(B) Learned behavioral tendencies of a young child

(C) Physical and emotional characteristics of a newborn child and young infant

(D) Psychological and physiological personality traits a young child models from his or her environment

(E) Emotional traits that infants outgrow by the time they turn two years old

316. Research has determined that, between the ages of 6 and 12 months, all babies have acquired:

(A) Three-dimensional dreaming

(B) The ability to walk

(C) The ability to talk

(D) Depth perception

(E) Potty-training abilities

317. Motor development in babies develops in a proximodistal fashion. This is best described as:

(A) From nearest to the center of the body to the farthest from the center

(B) From the top of the head to the bottom of the feet

(C) From the farthest from the center to the nearest to the center

(D) From the bottom of the body to the top of the body

(E) From the left of the body to the right of the body

318. Which of the following statements best defines maturation?

(A) It is directly based on social cognitive learning.

(B) It is the basis for all physiological and psychological development.

(C) It is an automatic biological development of the body and nervous system that naturally unfolds over time.

(D) It does not take place in all human beings.

(E) It is directly associated with genetic links.

319. According to Jean Piaget, at what stages of development are children able to grasp the concepts of object permanence and conservation, respectively?

(A) Formal operational; preoperational
(B) Concrete operational; formal operational
(C) Concrete operational; sensorimotor
(D) Sensorimotor; preoperational
(E) Sensorimotor; concrete operational

320. Jean Piaget defined egocentrism as:

(A) The belief that young adults don't listen to their parents
(B) The idea that preschool children cannot see things from another's point of view
(C) The understanding that young children cannot learn outside of a structured classroom
(D) The idea that young children are selfish and grow out of it over time
(E) The belief that children cannot do more than one task at a time

321. According to Jean Piaget, what type of learning do individuals acquire during the formal operational stage?

(A) Abstract thought
(B) Symbolism
(C) Memorization skills
(D) Visual learning
(E) Auditory learning

322. I developed an experimental procedure in order to observe the variety of attachment forms exhibited between mothers and infants. Called the "Strange Situation" method, it is based on a series of brief separations and reunions with the mother in a playroom situation. Who am I?

(A) Harry Harlow
(B) James Marcia
(C) Mary Ainsworth
(D) Carol Gilligan
(E) Diana Baumrind

323. According to Jean Piaget, children understand the concept of symbolism during which stage of development?

(A) Sensorimotor
(B) Preoperational
(C) Concrete operational
(D) Formal operational
(E) Operational

324. One major difference between assimilation and accommodation is that assimilation:

(A) Is a process by which children use old methods to deal with new situations
(B) Is a process by which children change their thought process to meet the needs of their world
(C) Is a process by which children gain an understanding of the world around them
(D) Is a process by which individuals shape their lives based on learned observations
(E) Is a process by which individuals begin using hypothetical thinking skills

325. According to Lawrence Kohlberg, during the preconventional stage of moral development children tend to:

(A) Base individual judgments on self-chosen principles
(B) Internalize the moral standards of valued adult role models
(C) Understand morality based on customs or values
(D) Interpret behavior in terms of concrete consequences
(E) Define good behavior as that which pleases other people

326. During a discussion in class regarding cheating in school, a student argues, "Cheating is wrong; it is important to follow rules." Lawrence Kohlberg would say this student is in what stage of moral development?

(A) Preconventional
(B) Conventional
(C) Postconventional
(D) Nonconventional
(E) Advanced conventional

327. As a preschooler, Emma has developed a number of cognitive and social skills that she will use to plan activities, accomplish tasks, and face challenges. According to Erik Erikson, what stage of psychosocial development is Emma in?

(A) Trust versus mistrust
(B) Autonomy versus self-doubt
(C) Initiative versus guilt
(D) Industry versus inferiority
(E) Identity versus role confusion

328. When Daniel begins walking, talking, and exploring, he is bound to get into conflict with his parents. If his parents punish his explorations, Daniel may develop a feeling that independence is bad. According to Erik Erikson, what stage of psychosocial development would this occur in?

(A) Identity versus role confusion
(B) Industry versus inferiority
(C) Initiative versus guilt
(D) Autonomy versus self-doubt
(E) Trust versus mistrust

329. According to Sigmund Freud, what is the correct order of the five psychosexual stages of development?

(A) Oral, anal, phallic, early, genital
(B) Oral, anal, phallic, latency, genital
(C) Anal, phallic, latency, genital, oral
(D) Genital, oral, latency, phallic, anal
(E) Phallic, anal, oral, latency, genital

330. If individuals successfully solve their problems during each stage of life, they will develop good social traits. If they do not, their problem-solving skills will be hindered, causing new problems at the next stage. Which psychologist(s) would agree with this statement?

(A) Freud
(B) Piaget
(C) Erikson
(D) A and B
(E) A and C

331. Monica is extremely neat and orderly. She cannot stand it when people touch things on her desk. She also has a problem lending money to even her closest friends. Freud would say she is stuck in what psychosexual stage?

(A) Oral
(B) Anal
(C) Phallic
(D) Latency
(E) Genital

332. Jenna is extremely sarcastic. She uses this to cover up her low self-esteem. Freud would say she is stuck in which psychosexual stage?

(A) Oral
(B) Anal
(C) Phallic
(D) Latency
(E) Genital

333. If a child believes stealing in order to save a life is OK because life is even more important than following the law, this child would be in what stage of moral development?

(A) Level one: preconventional
(B) Level two: conventional
(C) Level three: postconventional
(D) Level four: operational
(E) Level five: formal operational

334. Which of the following statements is a major criticism of Jean Piaget's work with cognitive development?

(A) Piaget failed to include clear age differences for his stages.
(B) Piaget placed too much emphasis on cognitive differences between young children and adolescents.
(C) Piaget often overestimated the cognitive abilities of children.
(D) Piaget often underestimated the cognitive abilities of children.
(E) Piaget gave little credit to other psychologists who helped him develop his theory.

335. When an infant opens her mouth and turns her head when touched on the cheek, this is indicative of the:

(A) Babinski reflex
(B) Moro reflex
(C) Rooting reflex
(D) Tonic reflex
(E) Attention reflex

336. Harry Harlow's experiment with monkeys and surrogate mothers emphasized the importance of:

(A) Satisfying hunger
(B) Body temperature
(C) Fulfilling needs
(D) Intrinsic motivation
(E) Contact

CHAPTER 17

Developmental Psychology: Adolescence and Adulthood

337. When adolescents were asked about their major concerns for their future, top answers on their lists were getting married, having friends, getting a job, and doing well in school. According to Jean Piaget, what stage of cognitive learning is this?

(A) Sensorimotor
(B) Preoperational
(C) Operational
(D) Formal operational
(E) Postoperational

338. When developing his model for moral reasoning, Kohlberg asked children, adolescents, and adults whether a person should steal medicine to save the life of a loved one. Which response represents conventional morality?

(A) Stealing the medicine is wrong because you could be punished.
(B) Stealing the medicine is right because you will be a hero by saving your loved one's life.
(C) Stealing the medicine is wrong because your friends will think you are a thief.
(D) Stealing the medicine is acceptable if it will save someone's life.
(E) Stealing the medicine is wrong under all circumstances.

339. Which of the following examples best illustrates a personal fable?
- (A) Talia feels insecure when she is making her presentation in front of her class.
- (B) Lola feels as though no one else could possibly be so much in love as she is.
- (C) Dina lies to her parents about going to her boyfriend's birthday party.
- (D) Alexa is no longer interested in her schoolwork; all she wants to do is hang out with her friends.
- (E) Joanna falls into a severe depression when her boyfriend breaks up with her.

340. Authoritative parents can best be defined as:
- (A) Parents who befriend their children and do not use discipline
- (B) Parents who are less controlling and behave with a more accepting attitude
- (C) Parents who try to control the behavior of their children in accordance with a set standard of conduct
- (D) Supportive parents who discuss their rules and policies with their children
- (E) Parents who command obedience and teach their values with little communication

341. According to Erik Erikson, what is one major conflict teenagers deal with during the identity versus role confusion stage of psychosocial development?
- (A) Finding a more purposeful life as an adult
- (B) Achieving personal satisfaction
- (C) Reflecting on previous life challenges
- (D) Finding intimacy by developing loving relationships
- (E) Achieving generativity through family relationships

342. Romantic love typically changes as time passes and goes through two phases. Which of the following best describes the passionate love stage of romantic love?
- (A) Deep, affectionate attachment
- (B) Feelings of trust, calmness, and bonding
- (C) An aroused state of intense positive absorption
- (D) Higher levels of oxytocin
- (E) Lower levels of oxytocin

343. Carol Gilligan believed moral decision making is dependent primarily on which of the following?

(A) Age
(B) Culture
(C) Religion
(D) Gender
(E) Nationality

344. All of Mary and John's children have turned out to be socially responsible adults. Which parenting style did Mary and John most likely use?

(A) Authoritarian
(B) Authoritative
(C) Permissive
(D) Autocratic
(E) Sensitive

345. A failure to develop a consistent identity results in:

(A) Role confusion
(B) Inferiority
(C) Insecurity
(D) Stagnation
(E) Social isolation

346. According to Erikson, teachers, friends, and other people outside of the home first become important in shaping attitudes of a child during what psychosocial stage?

(A) Autonomy versus self-doubt
(B) Initiative versus guilt
(C) Industry versus inferiority
(D) Integrity versus despair
(E) Trust versus mistrust

347. Which of the following attributes does *not* contribute to successful aging?

(A) An optimistic outlook
(B) Appropriate nutrition
(C) Support from family and friends
(D) Having two or more children
(E) Cultural respect for aging

348. According to Erikson, a child who is learning the importance of academic success in school based on receiving a report card is in what psychosocial stage?

(A) Industry versus inferiority
(B) Generativity versus stagnation
(C) Identity versus role confusion
(D) Initiative versus guilt
(E) Integrity versus despair

349. I am in my early fifties. If I do not reach out to others, especially young people, Erik Erikson says I will experience:

(A) Shame
(B) Depression
(C) Isolation
(D) Stagnation
(E) Despair

350. According to Lawrence Kohlberg, behavior directed by self-accepted moral principles is an example of what stage of moral development?

(A) Preconventional
(B) Conventional
(C) Postconventional
(D) Nonconventional
(E) Unconventional

351. According to Erik Erikson, as a young adult you are most interested in developing:

(A) Initiative
(B) Integrity
(C) Generativity
(D) Trust
(E) Intimacy

352. Which group of stages from Erikson, Kohlberg, and Levinson identify the same phase of life?

(A) Identity, conventional, age 50 crisis
(B) Generativity, postconventional, age 50 crisis
(C) Generativity, preconventional, midlife transition
(D) Intimacy, preconventional, midlife transition
(E) Initiative, conventional, age 30 crisis

353. According to Freud, adolescents are in what psychosexual stage?

(A) Oral

(B) Anal

(C) Phallic

(D) Latency

(E) Genital

354. Which three stages best match the stage of development birth to 1.5 years of age according to Freud, Erikson, and Piaget?

(A) Anal, autonomy versus shame and doubt, preoperational

(B) Phallic, initiative versus guilt, concrete operations

(C) Oral, trust versus mistrust, sensorimotor

(D) Oral, identity versus role confusion, concrete operations

(E) Intimacy, generativity, ego integrity

355. Jack and Jill have entered elementary school, and both find spelling difficult. Jill's parents help her with her lessons and encourage her while Jack's parents show little interest in helping him. According to Erikson, this scenario is most likely to have an effect on what stage of the children's development?

(A) Trust versus mistrust

(B) Autonomy versus doubt

(C) Initiative versus guilt

(D) Industry versus inferiority

(E) Identity versus role confusion

356. At the age of 40, Daniel is single and works as a sports photographer. He doesn't own a home and lives in an outfitted camper van so he can travel around the country to meet with clients. His parents are worried that Daniel has not found a wife or bought a home at his age. What concept describes Daniel's parents' concerns?

(A) Social identity

(B) Emerging adulthood

(C) Intimacy

(D) Social clock

(E) Delayed adulthood

CHAPTER 18

Developmental Psychology: Death and Dying

357. Claire just celebrated her 90th birthday with her family and close friends. According to Erik Erikson, she has probably achieved:

(A) Isolation
(B) Integrity
(C) Despair
(D) Autonomy
(E) Stagnation

358. Which is the correct order of the five stages of dealing with death or loss?

(A) Denial, anger, bargaining, depression, acceptance
(B) Anger, denial, bargaining, depression, acceptance
(C) Bargaining, anger, denial, depression, acceptance
(D) Depression, bargaining, anger, denial, acceptance
(E) Depression, anger, denial, bargaining, acceptance

359. Which of the following psychologists formulated a stage theory addressing our encounters with grief?

(A) Sigmund Freud
(B) Erik Erikson
(C) Elisabeth Kübler-Ross
(D) Carol Gilligan
(E) Lawrence Kohlberg

360. In late adulthood, individuals experience a decrease in which of the following?

(A) Sexual desire
(B) Cognitive abilities
(C) Creativity
(D) Intellect
(E) Compassion for others

361. Ethel, who is 80 years old, lost her husband last year, and her children hardly ever come to visit. She looks back on her life with a lot of regret. According to Erik Erikson she is experiencing:

(A) Stagnation
(B) Depression
(C) Regression
(D) Despair
(E) Isolation

CHAPTER 19

Freudian Psychology

362. Freud's psychodynamic theory of personality emphasizes:

(A) The importance of early childhood experiences
(B) The importance of sibling rivalries
(C) The role genetics plays in personality development
(D) The nature-nurture debate
(E) The conscious thought process only

363. Rita is unable to stay in a long-term relationship but always has a rational explanation for ending the relationship that, to her friends, does not seem rational at all. According to Freud, Rita is likely ending all her relationships because of:

(A) Conscious forces
(B) Subconscious tendencies
(C) Unconscious motivation
(D) Preconscious motivation
(E) Conscious association

364. A psychologist reads a list of words to his client, who immediately responds with the first thing that comes to mind. This technique is best described as:

(A) Unconscious motivation
(B) Free association
(C) Free analysis
(D) Freudian interpretation
(E) Psychodynamic theory

365. Freud believed the mental process must have a source of primitive energy called:

(A) Ego

(B) Superego

(C) Id

(D) Conscious

(E) Unconscious

366. As children learn they must follow rules and regulations in satisfying their wishes, they develop:

(A) A superego

(B) An id

(C) An ego

(D) A preconscious

(E) An unconscious

367. Young children discover that their parents put restrictions on satisfying their desires. As a result, they learn to control their impulses and satisfy their desires in a socially acceptable manner. According to Freud, they do this through the development of:

(A) An id

(B) A superego

(C) An ego

(D) A conscious

(E) A subconscious

368. Which of the following examples best illustrates the pleasure principle?

(A) A student takes pleasure in reporting a fellow classmate for cheating.

(B) A new mother breastfeeds her infant.

(C) A corporate executive takes a vacation after working extremely hard the past month.

(D) A spoiled child acts out by throwing his toys at the wall when he doesn't get the Christmas gift he wanted.

(E) A mother and father fight about whether their son should have the privilege of staying out late to attend a party.

369. A defense mechanism is best defined by Freud as:

(A) A systematic process used to avoid confrontation
(B) A thought process that operates at an unconscious level to help an individual reduce anxiety
(C) The creation of acceptable excuses for unacceptable behavior
(D) The transfer of feelings from the unconscious to the conscious
(E) A thought process by which forbidden desires are acknowledged

370. Todd has had a crush on Donna for the past year, but he does not have the courage to ask her out. He is frustrated with himself and begins taking a kickboxing class at his local gym. This scenario best illustrates which defense mechanism?

(A) Displacement
(B) Projection
(C) Reaction formation
(D) Rationalization
(E) Sublimation

371. Which of the following statements best illustrates rationalization?

(A) Jay fails his math class and blames it on his teacher not liking him.
(B) After fighting with her best friend, Annie starts an argument with her mother.
(C) Janie feels so guilty about cheating, she confesses to her teacher.
(D) Conner is a heavy smoker but disregards all the evidence that says smoking can kill you.
(E) Jarred doesn't want to believe that his pastor could have molested his younger brother.

372. Tom is still in love with his girlfriend, who broke up with him last week, but he acts as if he doesn't care and is actually happy to be rid of her. This is an example of which of the following defense mechanisms?

(A) Regression
(B) Projection
(C) Sublimation
(D) Displacement
(E) Reaction formation

373. According to Freud, what is the preconscious?

(A) Another name for "conscious"

(B) The opposing force for the unconscious

(C) The part of the mind that is right below the conscious surface

(D) The part of the mind that works directly with the id

(E) The part of the unconscious that does not hold repressed desires

374. According to Freud, in what stage of psychosexual development does the Oedipus complex take place?

(A) Oral

(B) Anal

(C) Latency

(D) Phallic

(E) Genital

375. The female version of the Oedipus complex is called the:

(A) Victoria complex

(B) Isabella complex

(C) Pleasure complex

(D) Electra complex

(E) Octavia complex

376. According to Freud's psychosexual theory of development, a man's repression of sexual urges is a result of which of the following?

(A) Fixation in the latency stage

(B) Fixation in the oral stage

(C) Fixation in the anal stage

(D) Fixation in the genital stage

(E) Fixation in the phallic stage

377. One major criticism of Freudian psychoanalytic theory is that it:

(A) Focuses too much attention on sexual conflicts and fixations

(B) Assumes all behaviors are learned during childhood

(C) Is too pessimistic about the future of humanity

(D) Focuses too much attention on the id and not enough on the ego

(E) Gives too much power to conscious behavior

378. A three-year-old boy is rejecting his father and only wants to be around his mother. Freud would theorize the child is going through which phase?

(A) Electra complex
(B) Pleasure principle
(C) Oedipus complex
(D) Reality principle
(E) Latency period

379. Grace realizes she got back an extra hundred dollars from the bank teller. She has to decide whether or not she should return to the bank and inform the bank teller of the mistake. Grace is currently in conflict between her:

(A) Conscious and unconscious
(B) Id and superego
(C) Ego and superego
(D) Preconscious and unconscious
(E) Id and conscious

380. A fixation in the oral stage will include all of the following behaviors except:

(A) Overeating
(B) Low self-esteem
(C) Sarcasm
(D) Self-consciousness
(E) Aggressiveness

381. James has been divorced twice. Now anytime he even goes out on a date with women, they tell him he is very misogynistic. James could be fixated in what psychosexual stage of development?

(A) Oral
(B) Anal
(C) Phallic
(D) Latency
(E) Genital

CHAPTER 20

Personality Psychology

382. The "anima," "animus," "persona," and "shadow" are all:

(A) Archetypes in the collective unconscious according to Carl Jung
(B) Parts of the drive for superiority according to Alfred Adler
(C) Components of Karen Horney's beliefs on neurotic needs
(D) Terms used by Sigmund Freud to explain the Oedipus complex
(E) Roles encouraged by neo-Freudians

383. Which theory of personality emphasizes the value and importance of unconditional positive regard with regard to relationships?

(A) Psychoanalytic psychology
(B) Humanistic psychology
(C) Cognitive psychology
(D) Developmental psychology
(E) Behavioral psychology

384. The "Big Five" personality characteristics are:

(A) Emotionality, extroversion, openness, neuroticism, and agreeableness
(B) Anxiety, extroversion, agreeableness, neuroticism, and sociability
(C) Outgoing, conscientiousness, extroversion, agreeableness, and neuroticism
(D) Openness, conscientiousness, extroversion, agreeableness, and neuroticism
(E) Extroversion, neuroticism, anxiety, agreeableness, and openness

385. Research shows that individuals with a type A personality are more prone to:

(A) Extroversion
(B) Cardiac health problems
(C) Poverty
(D) Sexual dysfunction
(E) Psychoticism

386. Which of the following statements is a good example of a Jungian archetype?

(A) Owen, who is 37, still wants to please his domineering mother.
(B) Erica does not want anyone to know she uses food stamps.
(C) George runs for class president because he wants his classmates to believe he is a confident person.
(D) Tanya consciously strives to become the best golf player on her team.
(E) Joan, who is haunted by her memories of child abuse, seeks help by going to a psychotherapist.

387. Which of the following tests is an example of a projective test, consisting of a set of ambiguous pictures about which people are asked to tell a story?

(A) MMPI-2
(B) Rorschach
(C) LSAT
(D) TAT
(E) ASW

388. Which of the following terms does *not* describe the assumption behind Carl Rogers's self theory?

(A) Unconditional positive regard
(B) Congruency
(C) Self-actualization
(D) Empathic understanding
(E) Extroversion

389. According to Carl Rogers, a client's personality is determined by measuring the difference between:

(A) Introversion and extroversion
(B) Ideal self and real self
(C) Self-efficacy and self-esteem
(D) Persona and shadow
(E) Self-actualization and esteem needs

390. According to Albert Bandura, self-efficacy is best described as:

(A) The way in which an individual views his or her self-worth
(B) A voluntary decision to postpone a personal reward until a specific task is completed
(C) An individual's personal beliefs regarding how capable he or she is in controlling events and completing tasks
(D) An individual's social, political, and cultural views on issues that influence his or her learning potential
(E) An individual's beliefs about how much control he or she has over choices he or she has and decisions he or she makes

391. Ted believes that when he graduates depends primarily on his motivation and determination. This thought process is called:

(A) Self-efficacy
(B) Self-actualization
(C) Social cognition
(D) Internal locus of control
(E) External locus of control

392. Which of the following is a statistical method used to identify clusters of test items that relate to basic components of intelligence such as verbal skill?

(A) Empirical derivation
(B) Trait analysis
(C) Personality inventory
(D) Factor analysis
(E) Personality analysis

393. The trait theory can best be defined as:

(A) The analysis of how much personality or behavioral traits are influenced by genetics

(B) The analysis of the structure of personality by classifying similarities and differences in personality characteristics

(C) A factor analysis that studies common personality characteristics

(D) The organization of personality traits using specific categories to describe all characteristics

(E) Grouping individual behaviors based on interactions between particular personality characteristics

394. A true-false self-report questionnaire that describes a wide range of normal and abnormal behaviors is called:

(A) Thematic Apperception Test

(B) Validity Test

(C) Rorschach Test

(D) Objective Personality Test

(E) Minnesota Multiphasic Personality Inventory

395. The _____ theory minimized the role of the unconscious.

(A) Humanistic

(B) Trait

(C) Psychoanalytic

(D) Behaviorist

(E) Functionalist

396. Mary always assumed that improving physical strength was something only men could do. However, after observing women body builders, Mary began to believe that she could start lifting weights. This is an example of a belief being created through:

(A) Outcome expectancy

(B) Distortion of consequences

(C) Self-esteem

(D) Self-efficacy

(E) Self-confidence

397. Alfred Adler proposed that humans are motivated by:

(A) Conscious drives
(B) Neurotic needs
(C) Empathic understanding
(D) Social urges
(E) Intrinsic motivation

398. Which of the following neo-Freudians believed that the major influence on personality development is found in the child-parent social interaction?

(A) Adler
(B) Horney
(C) Jung
(D) Rogers
(E) Bandura

399. When Johnny comes home from school and appears to be angry, his mother, Mary, wonders whether it is because of Johnny's notoriously bad temper or because someone was mean to Johnny. A psychologist studying how Mary tries to explain Johnny's behavior would likely be using which of the following?

(A) Attribution theory
(B) Self-efficacy theory
(C) Behavioral theory
(D) Trait theory
(E) Social learning theory

400. Neo-Freudians agree with Freud on all of the following basic ideas except:

(A) Importance of the unconscious
(B) The division of the mind
(C) The use of defense mechanisms
(D) The importance of sexual drives and conflicts
(E) The protection of the ego

401. The importance of our capacity for personal growth, development of our potential, and freedom to choose our destiny is the emphasis of which psychological theory?

(A) Psychoanalytic psychology
(B) Existentialism
(C) Behaviorism
(D) Humanism
(E) Cognitive psychology

402. Radical determinism is to behaviorism as _____ is to the social-cognitive theory.

(A) Psychological determinism
(B) Rational determinism
(C) Reciprocal determinism
(D) Evolutionary determinism
(E) Environmental determinism

403. Liz is getting ready for a blind date and is nervous about the impression and signals she may give to her date as well as how she will interpret the signals given by her date, especially after watching a film about date rape. If a psychologist were studying Liz's thought processes, what area of psychology would best be applied for the study?

(A) Biopsychology
(B) Social cognition psychology
(C) Developmental psychology
(D) Social psychology
(E) Behavioral psychology

CHAPTER 21

Stress and Coping

404. Stress is best defined as:

(A) A subjective evaluation of a situation that we believe to be overwhelming

(B) A threatening feeling that comes when we interpret a situation as more than our psychological or physiological resources can handle

(C) A potentially harmful situation from which we can potentially sustain some harm or damage

(D) A situation that we see as a challenge to our psyche

(E) A measure of how much we can handle a potentially threatening situation

405. Lamar was asked to give blood. He has a terrible fear of doing so. He automatically thinks this will have negative effects on his well-being. This is an example of what type of appraisal?

(A) Harm/loss

(B) Challenge

(C) Threat

(D) Stress

(E) Negative

406. Which of the following statements is true regarding the fight-flight response?

(A) It can be triggered by physical stimuli that threaten our survival.

(B) It directs a great source of energy from the brain to the muscles.

(C) It calms the body down after the response to a stress stimulus has occurred.

(D) It stimulates the thyroid gland to release a stress hormone called adrenaline.

(E) It automatically reduces physiological stress triggers by slowing down the heart rate.

407. Physical symptoms such as headaches, muscle pain, and stomach problems brought on by psychological factors like worry and tension are called:

(A) Resistance symptoms
(B) Prolonged stress symptoms
(C) Psychological symptoms
(D) Psychosomatic symptoms
(E) Appraisal symptoms

408. Stress appraisal stimulates which part of the brain?

(A) Thalamus
(B) Hypothalamus
(C) Amygdala
(D) Cerebrum
(E) Medulla

409. When the adrenal medulla is activated by the sympathetic nervous system, _____ is secreted.

(A) Epinephrine
(B) Dopamine
(C) Serotonin
(D) Acetylcholine
(E) Glycogen

410. What are the three stages of the general adaptation syndrome (GAS)?

(A) Alarm, fight, relaxation
(B) Alarm, control, exhaustion
(C) Resistance, alarm, homeostasis
(D) Alarm, resistance, exhaustion
(E) Resistance, exhaustion, relaxation

411. Which of the following examples best illustrates frustration?

(A) A basketball coach loses his temper when his team loses a game they should have won.
(B) Two wolves fight to become the leader of the pack.
(C) A child starts crying when his mother says goodbye to him in preschool.
(D) A spider eats a fly.
(E) A farmer kills a chicken to eat for dinner.

412. When we balance the demands of a potentially stressful situation with our ability to meet these demands, it is called:

(A) Secondary appraisal

(B) Threat appraisal

(C) Harm/loss appraisal

(D) Challenge appraisal

(E) Primary appraisal

413. Eva's professor keeps telling her how the tests and quizzes she takes in his class are opportunities to demonstrate her understanding of the material. Eva's professor is attempting to elicit what kind of appraisal?

(A) Harm/loss

(B) Threat

(C) Challenge

(D) Primary

(E) Secondary

414. What effect do harm/loss appraisals have that challenge appraisals do *not* have?

(A) Lower physiological arousal

(B) Higher levels of negative emotions

(C) More psychological stimulation

(D) A triggering of physiological arousal

(E) Increased activity of the parasympathetic nervous system

415. In what stage of the general adaptation syndrome is there a breakdown to internal organs and a weakening of the immune system?

(A) Alarm

(B) Resistance

(C) Exhaustion

(D) Relaxation

(E) Negative

416. Just before her solo at her chorus concert, Charlene's heart begins to race and her face becomes flushed. According to Hans Selye, Charlene is in what stage of stress?

(A) Alarm
(B) Resistance
(C) Exhaustion
(D) Primary
(E) Psychosomatic

417. Which of the following is *not* an example of a major source of stress?

(A) Hassles
(B) Change
(C) Pressure
(D) Frustration
(E) Fear

418. Richard Lazarus's theory on stress emphasizes which of the following as the first step in experiencing stress?

(A) Fear
(B) Threat
(C) Flight
(D) Appraisal
(E) Anger

CHAPTER 22

Disorders

419. Lee is unable to tell the difference between right and wrong in any aspect of his life. This statement is describing which type of abnormal behavior?

(A) Depression
(B) Maladaptive
(C) Insanity
(D) Anxiety
(E) Psychotic

420. The learning perspective states that the main cause of mental disorders is:

(A) Reinforcement of maladaptive behavior learned through experience
(B) Irrational thought processes
(C) Internal conflict from one's childhood
(D) Low self-esteem
(E) Chemical imbalance in the brain

421. DSM-V was designed to help with which of the following?

(A) Identifying psychological disorders
(B) Identifying the causes of psychological disorders
(C) Classifying psychological disorders
(D) Listing venues where individuals can diagnose their disorder
(E) Distinguishing between sanity and insanity

422. A somatoform disorder can best be defined as:

(A) Disorder in which hallucinations occur often

(B) Disorder in which an individual experiences extreme anxiety

(C) Disorder in which symptoms are completely made up by the individual

(D) Disorder in which symptoms are produced by psychological factors

(E) Disorder in which an individual has delusional thoughts

423. Which of the following examples best illustrates a person with obsessive-compulsive disorder (OCD)?

(A) Steven hyperventilates whenever he is in an elevator.

(B) Shelly complains constantly about feeling sick and goes to many doctors.

(C) Bari is extremely anxious and panics every time she gets on an airplane.

(D) Blake wanders around town in a daze, not sure how she got there.

(E) Adam must lock his door 10 times before he leaves for work every morning.

424. A soldier experiences sudden blindness after returning from battle. He would most likely be diagnosed with which of the following disorders?

(A) Conversion disorder

(B) Dissociative disorder

(C) Bipolar disorder

(D) Hypochondriac

(E) A phobic disorder

425. Which of the following disorders is *not* an anxiety disorder?

(A) Agoraphobia

(B) Panic

(C) PTSD

(D) Selective mutism

(E) Specific phobia

426. This disorder is characterized by irritability, difficulty concentrating, and inability to control one's worry.

(A) Phobias
(B) Generalized anxiety
(C) Obsessive-compulsive
(D) Bipolar
(E) Attention deficit hyperactivity disorder

427. A patient describes having frequent episodes that come on suddenly and last for several minutes. During the episodes, the patient feels dizzy, has trouble breathing, and thinks her heart might explode. The threat of these episodes gives the patient significant anxiety. The patient's symptoms indicate that she is suffering from:

(A) Bipolar disorder
(B) Panic disorder
(C) Schizophrenia
(D) Obsessive-compulsive disorder
(E) Personality disorder

428. Which of the following symptoms is *not* a symptom of obsessive-compulsive disorder?

(A) Irrational thoughts
(B) Impulsive behavior
(C) Uncontrollable images
(D) Severe depression
(E) Ritualized behavior

429. Individuals who have reported paralysis of a limb, blindness, or seizures with no physical or neurological damage are most likely suffering from:

(A) A conversion disorder
(B) A panic disorder
(C) Posttraumatic stress disorder
(D) Hypochondriasis
(E) Bipolar disorder

430. Johnny is a young child who is constantly talking at home with his parents and siblings and with his friends outside of school. But when asked to speak in the classroom, whether it is giving a presentation or just answering a question about the lesson, Johnny consistently fails to respond. This type of anxiety disorder is known as:

(A) Selective mutism
(B) Panic disorder
(C) Generalized anxiety disorder
(D) Social anxiety disorder
(E) Separation anxiety disorder

431. After surviving a very severe car crash with only minor injuries, Taylor has had trouble sleeping almost every night. He has dreams in which he relives the car crash. During the day, Taylor has intrusive thoughts about the accident, leaving him with a racing heart. He has been avoiding driving and being in cars as much as possible. When he's with his friends and family, he feels detached and irritable, and is easily startled. Which disorder does this describe?

(A) Obsessive-compulsive disorder
(B) Posttraumatic stress disorder
(C) Major depressive disorder
(D) Social anxiety disorder
(E) Insomnia

432. Data suggest that the most common mental disorder is:

(A) Substance abuse
(B) Mood disorders
(C) Personality disorders
(D) Somatoform disorders
(E) Psychosexual disorders

433. Which of the following treatments is most often used to help clients who suffer from obsessive-compulsive disorder?

(A) Avoidance therapy
(B) Psychoanalysis
(C) Exposure therapy
(D) Biochemical treatment
(E) Cognitive behavioral therapy, or CBT, combined with medication

434. Some significant changes were made from DSM-IV to DSM-V. Which one of the following changes was made?

(A) All subtypes of schizophrenia were removed from the DSM-V.

(B) Gambling disorder and tobacco use disorder were removed from DSM-5.

(C) DSM-5 places greater emphasis on the multiaxial system of diagnosis.

(D) Social (pragmatic) communication disorder was removed from DSM-V.

(E) Premenstrual dysphoric disorder was added to an appendix for further study.

435. Mary's husband forgot their anniversary, leading Mary to think her husband does not love her anymore and to ultimately conclude that, because he does not love her, he hates her. This caused her to go into a rage and go to great lengths to ensure that her husband stays with her. What type of personality disorder does this scenario best represent?

(A) Borderline personality

(B) Narcissistic personality

(C) Histrionic personality

(D) Obsessive-compulsive personality

(E) Dependent personality

436. Gender-identity disorders involve:

(A) The use of unconventional sexual tendencies

(B) The desire to dress like individuals of the opposite sex

(C) Homosexual tendencies

(D) The rejection of one's biological gender

(E) The rejection of gender-related stereotypes

437. According to DSM-V, a personality disorder can be diagnosed when there are significant impairments in self and interpersonal functioning together with one or more pathological personality traits. In DSM-V, which one of the following general criteria for personality disorder must be met?

(A) One or more pathological personality trait domains or trait facets

(B) Avoidant behavior often accompanied by anxiety disorder

(C) Pattern stable, of long duration, and onset can be traced back at least to adolescence or early adulthood

(D) Enduring pattern not better accounted for as a manifestation or consequence of mental disorder

(E) Irritability and aggressiveness, as indicated by repeated physical fights or assaults

438. DSM-5 has declassified which of the following as a mental illness?

(A) Gender dysphoria

(B) Transgender gender dysphoria

(C) Homosexuality

(D) Delusional disorder

(E) Hysterical neurosis

CHAPTER 23

Mood Disorders and Schizophrenia

439. Which of the following disorders does *not* fall under a mood disorder?

(A) Dysthymic disorder
(B) Bipolar disorder
(C) Major depression
(D) Cyclothymic disorder
(E) Schizophrenia

440. Lilly is now 35 years old. She just started therapy because she feels "down in the dumps." While in therapy she realizes she has felt this way most of her life. She is most likely suffering from:

(A) Major depression
(B) Bipolar disorder
(C) Dysthymic disorder
(D) Generalized anxiety disorder
(E) Antisocial personality disorder

441. Antidepressant drugs work mainly because they raise the level of a single neurotransmitter called:

(A) Dopamine
(B) Epinephrine
(C) Norepinephrine
(D) Serotonin
(E) Glycogen

442. Which of the following characteristics is *not* a symptom of a personality disorder?

(A) Major depression
(B) Inflexibility
(C) Maladaptive traits
(D) Impaired functioning
(E) Great social and personal distress

443. Jeff has total disregard for the rights or properties of others. He steals all the time from just about anyone. He randomly harasses people. He has consistently destroyed his neighbor's property. Last month he was arrested for kidnapping. While in jail he continues to lie and have little remorse for his actions. Jeff is suffering from what mental disorder?

(A) Major depression
(B) Antisocial personality disorder
(C) Schizoid personality disorder
(D) Dependent personality disorder
(E) Paranoid personality disorder

444. Which of the following is *not* a symptom of major depressive disorder?

(A) Markedly diminished interest or pleasure in activities most of the day
(B) Fear or avoidance of situations, such as crowds, where one has feelings of loss of control and panic
(C) Problems in thinking, concentrating, or making decisions
(D) Problems regulating appetite
(E) Insomnia or sleeping too much

445. Which of the following characterizes paranoid personality disorder?

(A) Unstable moods
(B) Lack of social relationships
(C) Lack of conscience
(D) Inaccurate sense of self-worth
(E) Extreme suspiciousness and mistrust of other people

446. Early childhood sexual or physical abuse is a common feature among people suffering from:

(A) Somatoform disorder
(B) Dissociative identity disorder
(C) Bipolar disorder
(D) Major depression
(E) Schizophrenia

447. From the time he was a young child, Scott has had no problem lying to authority figures. As an adult he considers himself good with the ladies. He has little remorse for his maladaptive behavior. Scott would most likely be diagnosed with:

(A) Antisocial personality disorder
(B) Paranoid personality disorder
(C) Narcissistic personality disorder
(D) Schizoid personality disorder
(E) Schizophrenia

448. Priscilla spent the last four weeks in bed. Without telling her friends or family, she bought a $3,000 plane ticket to Europe. She took most of her savings with her to go on a major shopping spree when she gets there. Priscilla is most likely suffering from:

(A) Narcissistic personality disorder
(B) Major depression
(C) Schizoid personality disorder
(D) Bipolar disorder
(E) Dysthymic disorder

449. Excessive dopamine is to _____ as too little dopamine is to _____.

(A) Parkinson's disease, schizophrenia
(B) Schizophrenia, Parkinson's disease
(C) Antisocial personality disorder, schizoid personality disorder
(D) Depression, schizophrenia
(E) Schizophrenia, depression

450. All of the following are symptoms of schizophrenia except:

(A) Delusions

(B) Hallucinations

(C) Disorganized speech

(D) Manic behavior

(E) Decreased emotional expression

451. Which of the following is an example of a positive symptom of schizophrenia?

(A) Hallucinations

(B) Dulled emotions

(C) Little inclination to speak

(D) Loss of normal functions

(E) Intellectual impairment

452. This type of disorder is characterized by rigid and long-lasting behavior patterns that are disruptive. These behavior patterns diminish an individual's ability to successfully function in society. What type of disorder does this describe?

(A) Dissociative disorder

(B) Anxiety disorder

(C) Bipolar disorder

(D) Mood disorder

(E) Personality disorder

453. Khloe walked into a police station looking disheveled and confused. She could not remember her name, didn't recall where she came from, and couldn't remember anything about her past. Khloe has experienced:

(A) Dissociative amnesia

(B) Dissociative fugue

(C) Dissociative identity disorder

(D) Schizophrenia

(E) Antisocial personality disorder

454. Researchers have determined that there is a genetic marker in the development of schizophrenia. To test this theory, researchers used which of the following groups?

(A) Fraternal twins
(B) Siblings
(C) Parents and children
(D) Unrelated individuals
(E) Identical twins

455. Research suggests there is a direct correlation between the presence of major depression and:

(A) Moderate levels of dopamine
(B) Decreased levels of serotonin
(C) Increased levels of endorphins
(D) Enlarged hypothalamus
(E) Enlarged parietal lobe

456. Autistic spectrum disorders are considered to be:

(A) Developmental disorders
(B) Mood disorders
(C) Learning disabilities
(D) Personality disorders
(E) Dissociative disorders

457. Narcissistic personality disorder is characterized by:

(A) An unstable self-image
(B) Feelings of inadequacy
(C) Social isolation
(D) Inflated sense of self
(E) Compulsive tendencies

CHAPTER 24

Therapies

458. The analysis of a client's past experiences and suggestions for ways the client can overcome his or her problems that stem from these experiences is the basis for which type of therapy?

(A) Cognitive therapy
(B) Behavioral therapy
(C) Psychoanalytic therapy
(D) Developmental therapy
(E) Social-cognitive therapy

459. Which of the following examples best illustrates insight therapy?

(A) A client takes various psychoactive drugs to treat a mental disorder.
(B) A therapist and client work together with the goal of identifying the problem and reaching a possible solution.
(C) The therapist and client discuss key traumatic issues faced by the client in his or her childhood.
(D) The therapist combines various techniques from many different therapeutic approaches.
(E) The therapist focuses on the thoughts of the unconscious and brings these thoughts to the surface through dream analysis.

460. Which of the following is one major difference between a clinical psychologist and a psychiatrist?

(A) A psychiatrist uses biomedical treatment.
(B) A psychiatrist uses an eclectic approach.
(C) A psychiatrist cannot counsel clients.
(D) A psychiatrist recognizes the importance of group therapy.
(E) A psychiatrist treats clients in hospitals.

461. Joy's therapist is trying to encourage her to take charge of the therapy session. The therapist uses active listening while Joy discusses her feelings. Which therapy is most likely being described?

(A) Psychodynamic therapy
(B) Rational emotive therapy
(C) Existential therapy
(D) Cognitive-behavioral therapy
(E) Client-centered therapy

462. The antidepressant drug Prozac does which of the following?

(A) Blocks the reuptake of serotonin
(B) Blocks the reuptake of dopamine
(C) Levels the amount of epinephrine
(D) Deceases the amount of adrenaline in the bloodstream
(E) Decreases the level of acetylcholine in the bloodstream

463. Albert Ellis devised a therapy that can be very confrontational. The client must face the irrationality of his or her belief system. What is the name of this form of therapy?

(A) Cognitive-behavioral therapy
(B) Gestalt therapy
(C) Rational emotive therapy
(D) Insight therapy
(E) Social-cognitive therapy

464. An example of aversive therapy is:

(A) An operant conditioning therapy that uses negative reinforcement to continued behavior
(B) A classically conditioned therapy based on the theory that repeated pairings of negative effects lead to extinction
(C) Using generalization to let all negative behavior pairings occur
(D) Spontaneous recovery occurring long after a behavior that was based on negative pairing has ended
(E) The use of modeling behavior so clients can see the consequences of negative behaviors

465. Gestalt therapy includes which of the following?

(A) Free association
(B) Electroshock therapy
(C) Behavioral therapy
(D) Dream analysis
(E) Biomedical therapy

466. Which of the following best describes transference in psychotherapy?

(A) A client who struggles with anger and hostility toward his coworkers may find himself similarly struggling with anger and hostility toward the therapist.
(B) A patient who is extremely organized repeatedly cancels or forgets therapy appointments.
(C) Patients are required to say whatever comes into their minds without holding back anything.
(D) A patient suggests events or feelings that will surely happen or are already happening.
(E) A patient has adulterous feelings and accuses his or her partner of infidelity.

467. Which of the following is a major goal of Aaron Beck's cognitive therapy?

(A) To rid an individual of his or her internal negative thought process
(B) To change an individual's negative behavior
(C) To enable a person to become self-actualized
(D) To stop individuals from using selective attention
(E) To help a client change learned or modeled behavior

468. Jana wants to be a doctor when she grows up, but she has one serious problem: she is terribly afraid of blood. Since she was a little girl, she has passed out at the mere sight of blood. To overcome this fear so that she can pursue her dream of becoming a doctor, her therapist exposes her to blood while trying to relax her. What type of therapy is this?

(A) Social-cognitive therapy
(B) Systematic desensitization
(C) Behavioral therapy
(D) Rational emotive therapy
(E) Extinction

469. One major difference between a humanistic therapist and a behavioral therapist is that:

(A) A behavioral therapist focuses on one's childhood.

(B) A humanistic therapist pays attention to uncovering unconscious conflict.

(C) A behavioral therapist can offer medication to her or his clients.

(D) A humanistic therapist focuses more on empathy and support for her or his clients.

(E) A behavioral therapist places all of the burden on the client for her or his own healing.

470. Rational emotive therapy was designed to:

(A) Teach clients relaxation techniques

(B) Explore the unconscious conflicts from a client's childhood

(C) Challenge the self-defeating thoughts of the client

(D) Use antidepressant medication to overcome depression

(E) Use free association to uncover unconscious thoughts and feelings

471. The purpose of free association is to:

(A) Help bring unconscious conflict to the surface

(B) Facilitate changing negative behaviors

(C) Change the client's thought process

(D) Rid an individual of his or her sexual desires

(E) Help a patient relax

472. Light therapy is used to help which of the following disorders?

(A) Major depression

(B) Dysthymic disorder

(C) Obsessive-compulsive disorder

(D) Dissociative identity disorder

(E) Seasonal affective disorder

473. Which of the following terms is *not* associated with psychoanalysis?

(A) Self-actualization

(B) Free association

(C) Dream analysis

(D) Hypnosis

(E) Sexual impulse

474. Which of the following psychologists believed that some people tend to have a pessimistic explanatory style, characterized by the tendency to blame bad events on themselves?

(A) Aaron Beck
(B) Martin Seligman
(C) Karen Horney
(D) Sigmund Freud
(E) Abraham Maslow

475. What is the name of the widely used therapy that involves giving an individual immediate information about the degree to which he or she can change anxiety-related responses, thereby improving control over his or her physiological process of arousal?

(A) Behavior modification
(B) Systematic desensitization
(C) Behavioral therapy
(D) Biofeedback
(E) Cognitive therapy

476. Which of the following therapies has been found effective in treating anxiety disorders, drug addictions, and autism?

(A) Psychoanalysis
(B) Social-cognitive therapy
(C) Behavioral therapy
(D) Biomedical feedback
(E) Gestalt therapy

CHAPTER 25

Social Psychology

477. John F. Kennedy's Bay of Pigs failure was caused in large part by:
   (A) Brainstorming
   (B) Group cohesion
   (C) Groupthink
   (D) Deindividuation
   (E) Diffusion of responsibility

478. Assuming that your culture's way of living is best, right, or natural in comparison to the culture of others is known as:
   (A) Prejudice
   (B) Ethnocentrism
   (C) Stereotype
   (D) Discrimination
   (E) Patronization

479. Whenever Danny aces a test, he thinks it is because he studied hard, but when he fails a test he thinks it's because the teacher did not explain the topics well enough. This is an example of:
   (A) Fundamental attribution error
   (B) Self-serving bias
   (C) Self schema
   (D) External attribution error
   (E) Person schema

480. The Stanford Prison experiment was a prime example of which of the following concepts?

(A) Conformity

(B) Compliance

(C) Obedience

(D) Cohesiveness

(E) Identification

481. According to the theory of cognitive dissonance, attitudes are changed because:

(A) We are rewarded by society when our beliefs coincide with the majority.

(B) Logical arguments compel us to alter our attitudes.

(C) Emotionally persuasive arguments motivate us to change our thought process.

(D) A state of tension motivates us to change our cognitive inconsistencies by making our beliefs more consistent.

(E) When our beliefs and behaviors are too similar it causes an unpleasant psychological state of tension.

482. Which of the following is an example of ethnocentrism?

(A) Believing that your culture's cuisine is the best.

(B) Refusing to date someone of another race.

(C) Believing that everyone from a certain region is a bad driver.

(D) Only working with people from your own culture.

(E) Feeling dislike for someone based on their ethnicity.

483. In Milgram's experiment, subjects who gave large shocks rationalized that they were not personally responsible for their actions. This raises questions about our willingness to commit inhumane acts as a result of:

(A) Coercive power

(B) Expert influence

(C) Obedience to authority

(D) Conformity to group pressure

(E) Individual compliance

484. Which of the following is *not* a characteristic of a collectivist culture?

(A) Social norms that promote selflessness
(B) Emphasis on working as a group
(C) Central role for families and communities
(D) Importance placed on doing what's best for society
(E) Emphasis on self-sufficiency

485. In a situation in which an individual is having a seizure on the street, helping could be inhibited by which of the following concepts?

(A) Groupthink
(B) Social comparison theory
(C) Risky shift
(D) Diffusion of responsibility
(E) Compliance

486. When making the "attribution error," we tend to overestimate the importance of _____ when judging the behaviors of others.

(A) Situational factors
(B) Personal factors
(C) Gender
(D) Intelligence
(E) Age

487. Through his experiments, Solomon Asch was able to demonstrate that:

(A) People will always conform in a group setting.
(B) Obedience to authority is determined by the perceived power of the authority figure.
(C) Size of majority does not influence how many people will conform.
(D) Compliance occurs in large groups.
(E) Lack of unanimity greatly reduces the pressure to conform.

488. One reason why many groups have some form of initiation rites and rituals is to have:

(A) Group norms
(B) Deindividuation
(C) Group cohesion
(D) Task-oriented groups
(E) Socially oriented groups

489. Jennifer wants to purchase a face cream to help moisturize and clear her skin. She sees two advertisements for different brands of face cream. One of the advertisements features her favorite actor and celebrity crush. Although the advertisements both mention similar features for each product, Jennifer decides to buy the cream that features the actor. This type of method to influence behavior is known as:

(A) Foot-in-the-door phenomenon
(B) Central route persuasion
(C) Peripheral route persuasion
(D) Cognitive dissonance
(E) Attribution theory

490. Damion rewrote his paper at the suggestion of his professor, even though he did not agree with the suggestions. This is an example of:

(A) Obedience
(B) Conformity
(C) Compliance
(D) Diffusion
(E) Cognitive dissonance

491. Which of the following scenarios is an example of deindividuation?

(A) Cindy finds that working in her group brings high levels of performance compared to students who work alone.
(B) Mindy forms a study group because she wants academic help, social support, and motivation.
(C) Amy has a poor running performance in competition; she performs even worse in front of a larger crowd.
(D) Torrie honks her horn loudly for quite a while because she has little chance of being personally identified.
(E) Jamie does not help the girl being attacked because the other byotanders are taking little action.

492. Mike has assured his mother that he will never get into a car with someone who has been drinking. But then he is out one night with a bunch of friends who have been drinking and he decides to come along for a ride with them after a long discussion. This change in Mike's judgment is known as:

(A) Risky shift
(B) Groupthink
(C) Group polarization
(D) Social comparison
(E) Group cohesion

493. Which of the following examples best illustrates a way to avoid groupthink from occurring?

(A) Choose a group captain to make all the final decisions.
(B) Allow the group's members the freedom to express differing opinions.
(C) Have every group member come in with a specific idea to bring to the table.
(D) Only allow one person in the group to speak at a time.
(E) Make the group socially oriented before making any final decisions.

494. Of the following examples, which would be the best example of self-serving bias?

(A) Michael, who believes that everyone should give to charities
(B) Paris, who believes she failed her math test even though she always gets an A in math
(C) Janet, who is always her teacher's favorite student
(D) Randy, who believes he works harder than others and is underappreciated
(E) Rebi, who overestimates her ability to run the after-school program for young children

495. Which of the following is *not* a characteristic of an individualistic culture?

(A) Importance placed on the uniqueness of each group member
(B) Emphasis on independence
(C) Social norms that promote autonomy
(D) Individual identity defined by relationships with others
(E) Central role of individual rights

496. David has always opposed the death penalty, believing it is not the place of the government to take the life of another person. After his best friend was murdered, David wanted nothing more than to see the murderer get the justice he or she deserved. Because the murder occurred in the state of Texas, this would mean justice would be served with the death penalty. The dissonance theory would state that:

(A) David would have no conflict in seeing the murderer put to death.

(B) David would have to change one of his attitudes to feel less tension.

(C) Justification of the death penalty would be appropriate in this situation.

(D) Morally, David would not support the death penalty under any circumstance.

(E) David would change his opinion in support of the death penalty.

497. John did poorly on a big test because it was too hot in the room and a student next to him was making distracting noises. John's friend also did poorly, which John attributes to his lack of study habits and failure to take notes. This is an example of:

(A) Self-fulfilling prophecy

(B) Actor-observer bias

(C) Dispositional attribution

(D) Attribution theory

(E) Just-world phenomenon

498. Evidence suggests that individuals tend to be attracted to others who are:

(A) Nearly opposite in all areas

(B) Similar to themselves in terms of perspective and values

(C) Physically more attractive than they are

(D) Unlikely to criticize or judge them

(E) Less intelligent than themselves

499. The tendency to "blame the victim" in a rape case is an example of which of the following terms?

(A) Fundamental attribution error
(B) Deindividuation
(C) Self-serving bias
(D) The just-world phenomenon
(E) Self-fulfilling prophecy

500. In the presence of the largest crowd she has ever seen, Heather gives her finest piano performance. This is an example of:

(A) Group cohesion
(B) Deindividuation
(C) Group polarization
(D) Social inhibition
(E) Social facilitation

501. According to the diffusion of responsibility theory, the biggest factor in predicting whether or not a bystander will help someone in need is:

(A) The duration of the situation
(B) Whether the person in need of help is male or female
(C) The number of other bystanders at the scene
(D) The level of perceived threat
(E) Whether the person actually asked for help

ANSWERS

Chapter 1: Schools of Thought

1. (A) Cognitive psychology is the study of how we process, store, and retrieve information. Choices (B) and (C) are devoted to studying the way people relate to others and the unique attributes of a person; neither field focuses on one's thought process. (D) deals with long-lasting changes in behavior, usually through experience. (E) is the experience of a meaningful pattern of a stimulus.

2. (C) Structuralism was an early school of psychological thought established by Titchener and Wundt at Cornell University in the 1890s. It sought to reveal the structural elements of the mind by engaging patients in self-reflective introspection.

3. (D) Wertheimer, along with Wolfgang Kohler and Kurt Koffka, studied the illusion of flashing lights and the perception of movement. Wertheimer argued that perceptual experiences, such as flashing lights, resulted from a "whole pattern" or, in German, "Gestalt."

4. (A) William James wrote *The Principles of Psychology*, published in 1890. This book included the study of the mind, sensation, memory, and reasoning. James is associated with functionalism. Wundt is associated with structuralism. Watson is associated with behaviorism. Freud is associated with psychoanalysis. Wertheimer is associated with Gestalt.

5. (A) John Watson published a paper called "Psychology as a Behaviorist Views It." Watson rejected the notion that introspection can be used as a technique to determine the behavior of human beings. Watson believed psychology needed to be an objective experimental science. Unlike choices (B), (C), (D), and (E), behaviorism was the first field to study psychology in an observable and measurable manner.

6. (D) The definition of the eclectic approach is a combination of techniques and ideas from many different schools of thought in psychology.

7. (D) The psychoanalytic approach focuses on the idea that each of us has an unconscious that contains thoughts, desires, and fears that have been hidden or repressed because they threaten our conscious self. (A), rewards and punishments, is based on behaviorism. (B), self-esteem and self-actualization, is based on humanism.

8. (A) In Pavlov's experiment in which he rang a bell before putting food in the dogs' mouths, the dogs eventually paired the bell with salivating, even when the food was not present. This phenomenon, which Pavlov called conditioned reflex, eventually became known as classical conditioning. Because this theory was based on involuntary reflexes and many psychologists believe human behavior is based on voluntary choices, they criticized classical conditioning, claiming it could not help us further understand human behavior. This explanation negates choice (C). Choices (D) and (E) are irrelevant to this question.

9. **(B)** William James pioneered functionalism, an early school of psychological thought that considered the function of consciousness. Functionalism focused on how our mental processes developed and adapted to contribute to our ancestors' survival.

10. **(B)** The behavioral approach analyzes how organisms learn or modify behavior based on rewards and punishments in the environment. The other choices do not specifically focus on reinforcements in one's environment.

11. **(D)** The behavioral approach emphasizes the objective, scientific analysis of observable behavior. This includes conditioning human behavior. Choice (A) focuses on an individual's thought process or perception. Choices (B) and (C) were both schools of thought that focused on introspection. Psychoanalysis emphasized the strength of the unconscious.

12. **(B)** Behaviorism redefined psychology as "the scientific study of observable behavior."

13. **(C)** Structuralism was influenced by the physical scientists of the time. Wundt emphasized that all complex substances could be separated into component elements, whereas functionalists examined behaviors from a different point of view. Functionalists were asking what the mind does and why. Choice (C) best exemplifies these concepts; (A) is too vague and inaccurate to be the correct answer; (B) does not represent either structuralism or functionalism; (D) is incorrect because both structuralism and functionalism used introspection as a means of determining human behavior. Once again, choice (E) is not using accurate information to define either structuralism or functionalism.

14. **(E)** The basis of humanism is the understanding that individuals have free will and a large capacity for reaching their potential. It is the human experience that we all share that enables individuals to attain such goals. Cognitive psychology is incorrect because it focuses on the process of thinking, perception, and attention to details of language and problem solving. Cognition does not emphasize the human experience. Structuralism focuses on complex mental elements. Behaviorism is based on relationships, stimulus-response, and rewards and punishments. Functionalists examined mental processes, not human experience.

15. **(A)** Psychoanalysis stresses the importance of the patient and psychologist working together to explore the client's past. Humanism emphasizes one's present

and future, not one's past. Cognitive psychology works on changing the client's way of thinking, again not placing much emphasis on the past. Eclectic simply means using several different approaches of psychology. Behavioral psychology tries to identify negative behaviors and eliminate them through such means as systematic desensitization.

16. **(D)** Psychodynamic psychology stresses the influence of the unconscious. Its fears, impulses, and desires motivate our conscious behavior. Choice (A), free will and self-actualization, refers to humanism. (B) refers to experimental psychology. (C) refers to part of Carl Jung's theory of personality development.

17. **(B)** Developmental psychologists study a person's biological, emotional, cognitive, and social development across the life span. Choice (A) is too vague to be the correct answer. (C) is incorrect because mental process refers to cognitive psychology, not developmental psychology. (D) and (E) are incorrect because they do not answer the question.

18. **(A)** Cognitive psychology is the scientific study of how we perceive, encode, process, store, and retrieve information. Cognitive psychologists are interested in how we think, use language, focus attention, remember, and problem solve.

19. **(C)** Biological psychologists focus on the ways changes in an organism's physical makeup can affect behavior, relating directly to genetics and the nervous system. Choices (A), (B), and (D) are incorrect because biological psychologists do not study the mind or life experiences. Choice (E) may appear to be correct, but the question is asking what the term *biological psychology* refers to, which is not drug treatment.

20. **(A)** Choice (A) is the definition for a case study. Choice (B) defines a longitudinal study. Choice (E) defines a cross-sectional study. Choices (C) and (D) do not define any type of study.

Chapter 2: Research Methods

21. **(D)** A correlation expresses a relationship between two variables without ascribing cause. Correlational research employs statistical methods to examine a relationship between two or more variables, but does not permit researchers to draw conclusions. Unlike correlational research, experimental research offers the opportunity to draw conclusions because of the strict control of variables.

22. **(A)** A random sample is defined as a sample in which each potential participant has an equal chance of selection. Choice (B) defines *representative sample*. Choice (C) defines the term *sample*, not *random sample*. Choices (D) and (E) do not accurately define *random sample*.

23. (C) While researchers were testing the hypothesis that better lighting would boost worker output in an electric plant in the 1920s, they were surprised to see their results showed something else entirely. Productivity increased regardless of lighting merely because of the researcher's attention and not factory conditions. Choice (A) is incorrect because the Hawthorne effect focuses on the researcher's attention, not expectations. Choice (B) refers to the researcher's bias and change of behavior, not the subject's.

24. (E) A confounding variable is anything that differs between the control group and the experimental group besides the independent variable. How fast and hungry the mice are at the beginning of the experiment are potential confounding variables. When and where the race takes place are also possible confounding variables that can potentially change the findings of this experiment. The population from which the mice were selected cannot be a confounding variable. This will not differ for the two groups. All of the mice were chosen from the same larger population. Even if this larger population is flawed, it is not considered a confounding variable.

25. (B) Marc has established a relationship. Marc did not conduct an experiment; therefore, he cannot draw any conclusions. Marc has found a correlation between studying and performance on a final exam; whether or not it is significant would require the use of inferential statistics.

26. (E) Jordan would need to use inferential statistics to determine whether the experimental group's aggression levels were significantly different. Jordan could very well use descriptive statistics, but not before he determines whether his hypothesis has been supported and represents the larger population.

27. (C) Correlational research allows the researcher to determine whether a relationship exists between two variables. A positive correlation means that high scores on one variable tend to be paired with high scores on the other variable. A number between -1 and +1 expresses the strength of the correlation. A negative correlation means that high scores on one variable tend to be paired with low scores on the other variable. The number 0 denotes the weakest possible correlation or no correlation at all.

28. (A) Standard deviation is a quantitative measure of how much a data set varies around the mean. The data sets have standard deviations of 7, 5, and 1, respectively. However, without the need for calculation, one can assess the relative variability in each data set by looking at the scores in each set. The first data set, [0, 0, 14, 14], contains scores that are relatively far from the mean of 7. Therefore, it will have the largest standard deviation. In contrast, the last data set, [6, 6, 8, 8], contains numbers that are relatively close to the mean of 7. Therefore, it will have the smallest standard deviation.

29. (B) The independent variable in the experiment is the variable that is manipulated to test its effects on the other, dependent variables. In this experiment, the manipulation of the number of alcoholic drinks given to the subjects will affect their levels of aggression. The dependent variable in the experiment is measured to see how it is changed from the manipulation of the independent variable.

30. (E) With an average height of 70 inches and a standard deviation of 3 inches, any height over 79 inches is more than 3 standard deviations away from the mean. Because height forms a normal distribution, this means than only 0.1% of men in the United States are likely to be taller than 79 inches.

31. (C) Statistically significant means a result is unlikely due to chance. It does not mean practical significance. Only by considering context can it be determined whether a difference is practically significant—that is, whether it requires action.

32. (B) A z-score, or standard score, indicates how many standard deviations an element is from the mean.

33. (E) For data sets that form a normal distribution or normal curve, such as those taken from typical intelligence tests, about 95 percent of the data points will fall within two standard deviations on either side of the mean. About 68 percent will fall within one standard deviation on either side of the mean.

34. (D) A skewed distribution denotes a data set in which the data points lack symmetry around the average. This contrasts with a normal distribution in which most of the data falls near the mean. In the example above, very few of the test scores were close to the mean of 70 percent; most were either much farther above or below the mean. Since the data points in this case lack symmetry around the average test score, this represents a skewed distribution.

35. (D) Although most scientists are pleased when their results confirm their hypothesis, research and observations should be performed from an objective viewpoint. Therefore, searching for results that confirm the initial hypothesis is not a part of the scientific method. Instead, this is an example of confirmation bias, the tendency to search for or interpret results in a way that confirms your preexisting beliefs.

36. (A) Naturalistic observation involves observing and recording behavior in a natural setting. The observer does not try to manipulate or control the situation in any way. The observer will systematically analyze the behavior that he or she has viewed. While naturalistic observations cannot explain behavior, the descriptive nature of this method can still be useful.

37. (D) Overconfidence (choice A), the tendency to find patterns in random events (choice B), and hindsight bias (choice C) are all reasons why the scientific method and other science-based approaches lead to more valid conclusions about the world around us as opposed to relying on common sense, intuition, or anecdotal evidence.

38. (B) Hindsight bias is the tendency to believe that you were certain of an outcome only after the outcome has already occurred. The effect is so strong that it can even cause distortions of our memories of what we knew or believed before an outcome occurred. This represents an important reason why science-based methods are needed to predict outcomes and draw conclusions about the natural world.

39. (A) Sampling bias is a flawed sampling process that creates an unrepresentative sample of a population. If you do not carefully choose study participants to be representative of your population of interest, your results and conclusions could be skewed and may not accurately reflect the population that you are studying.

40. (E) Both B and D represent weaknesses in Lisa's experimental design. By recruiting participants from volunteers that have responded to an advertisement, Lisa's experiment will not have a truly random sample that fairly represents the student population. Lisa used gender to choose which participants would make up her experimental and control groups. Groups should be randomly assigned to minimize any preexisting difference between the groups.

Chapter 3: The Brain

41. (E) The reticular formation arouses and alerts the forebrain and prepares it to receive information from all other senses. Damage to this location can cause permanent unconsciousness. Damage to the temporal lobe can cause speech and language issues. Damage to the frontal lobe can cause motivational and emotional issues. Damage to the parietal lobe can cause sensory motor issues.

42. (C) By measuring electrical impulses, an EEG (electroencephalogram) can detect epileptic seizures, covert processing, seizure disorders, and sleep disorders.

43. (B) The corpus callosum is a wide band of fibers that connect the left and the right hemispheres of the brain. It has 200 million neural fibers that allow information to pass back and forth between the hemispheres. It was believed that by cutting the corpus callosum, in what was known as a "splitbrain" operation, people suffering from epilepsy could decrease the number of seizures they had.

44. (A) The limbic system is a group of about half a dozen interconnected structures in the core of the forebrain that are involved in many motivational behaviors, such as eating, drinking, and sexual desire. Breathing regulations are controlled by the medulla. The cerebellum controls balance and coordination. Various regions in the left hemisphere of the brain control speech and language.

45. (A) The thalamus is often referred to as the "switchboard" of the brain. All sensory information that enters the brain goes through the thalamus. It is the job of the thalamus to relay the information to the appropriate region of the brain.

46. (D) The parietal lobe is located directly behind the frontal lobe. Its functions include processing sensory information from the body parts, which includes touching, locating limb positions, and feeling temperature. The occipital lobe is responsible for processing visual information. The temporal lobe is responsible for processing auditory information. The frontal lobe is responsible for interpreting and performing emotional behavior, behaving normally in social situations, and maintaining a healthy personality.

47. (B) Damage to the Broca's area will result in Broca's aphasia, which means a person cannot speak in fluent sentences but can understand written and spoken words.

48. (B) The occipital lobe is critical for recognizing objects. Damage to this area results in difficulties of recognition, a condition called visual agnosia. In visual agnosia the individual fails to recognize some object, person, or color, yet has the ability to see and describe parts of some visual stimuli.

49. (B) The patient will be able to say she saw the word ART because it was projected to the left hemisphere, which has the ability to control speech. Although the patient's right hemisphere saw the word HE, the right hemisphere turns out to be mute, meaning that it cannot say what it saw. However, the patient can point with her left hand to a photo of HE, indicating the right hemisphere understood the question.

50. (E) The somatosensory cortex is a narrow strip of the cortex that is located at the front edge of the parietal lobe. It processes sensory information about touch, location of limbs, pain, and temperature.

51. (C) The amygdala is involved in forming, recognizing, and remembering emotional experiences, unlike the hippocampus, which is responsible for transferring fleeting memories into permanent storage.

52. (A) An MRI, or magnetic resonance imaging, involves passing nonharmful radio frequencies through the brain. A PET scan, or positron emission tomography, involves injecting slightly radioactive solutions into the bloodstream.

53. (D) Regions A, B, C, and D in the diagram represent the frontal lobe, parietal lobe, occipital lobe, and temporal lobe, respectively. Together, these regions form the cerebral cortex, the outer layer of the cerebral hemispheres composed of millions of intricately interconnected neural cells. The cerebral cortex is the body's information-processing center.

54. (A) Region A represents the frontal lobe, which is part of the cerebral cortex. The frontal lobes are located directly behind the forehead. They are involved in speaking, muscle movements, and making plans and judgments.

55. (A) Region A represents the frontal lobe. The rear of the frontal lobes contains the motor cortex, the area of the brain that controls voluntary movements. Specific regions of the motor cortex control specific body parts such as legs, arms, fingers, and the face.

56. (D) Region D represents the temporal lobe. Located approximately above each ear, the temporal lobes contain the auditory regions of the brain. Each temporal lobe mainly receives information from the opposite ear.

57. (E) The area represented by E in the diagram is the medulla, or the base of the brainstem. The brainstem is the oldest and innermost region of the brain. The brainstem begins where the spinal cord expands slightly after entering the skull. The slightly expanded region is called the medulla, which controls heartbeat and breathing.

Chapter 4: Neuroscience

58. (A) Region A represents the cell body, or the soma of the neuron or nerve cell. This large structure contains the nucleus of the cell and supports the cell's ability to function.

59. (D) Region D represents the myelin sheath, a layer of fatty tissue that helps insulate the axon to make electrical impulses travel faster.

60. (C) Region C represents the neuron's axon, an extension that passes neural messages from the cell body to the terminal branches and on to other neurons, muscles, or glands.

61. (B) Region B represents the dendrites, densely packed fibers emanating from the neuron's cell body. The dendrites receive messages from surrounding neurons and transmit the message by conducting an electrical impulse toward the cell body.

62. (E) Region E represents the terminal branches of the neuron's axon. The axon terminals form junctions with other cells and transmit neural messages to nearby neurons, or to muscles or glands. While dendrites (region B) also interact with neighboring cells, they can only receive messages.

63. (D) The all-or-none law is the principle that the action potential in a neuron does not vary in strength; the neuron either fires at full strength or it does not fire at all. Choice (B) is incorrect because the synapse is the area composed of the axon terminal of one neuron and the dendrite of the next neuron. Choice (C) is incorrect because the resting state is when a neuron is positively charged outside and negatively charged on the inside. Choice (E) is incorrect because the sodium pump is a transport process that picks up sodium ions.

64. (C) Threatening or challenging physical or psychological stimuli trigger the sympathetic nervous system. This increases physiological arousal and prepares the body for action. The sympathetic nervous system prepares the body for "fight or flight." The parasympathetic nervous system helps return the body to equilibrium, also called homeostasis.

65. (B) Alcohol affects the nervous system in a number of ways, blocking some neural receptors and stimulating others. Some neurons are excited by the neurotransmitter GABA, which the brain normally manufactures. Alcohol molecules so closely resemble those of GABA neurotransmitters that alcohol can function like GABA and open GABA receptors. Anandamide is involved in memory, motor coordination, and emotions. Dopamine is critical to the way the brain controls movement; there is a direct link to dopamine levels in the body and Parkinson's disease and schizophrenia. Acetylcholine is a major excitatory neurotransmitter. Serotonin influences mood levels in the body.

66. (A) The sympathetic nervous system and parasympathetic nervous system are both subdivisions of the autonomic nervous system. The sympathetic nervous system prepares the body for threatening or challenging situations, which means increased blood pressure and increased heart rate. The parasympathetic nervous system returns the body to a relaxed state, for example, decreased heart rate.

67. (E) Efferent neurons carry information away from the spinal cord to produce responses in various muscles. Afferent neurons carry information from the senses to the spinal cord. Interneurons carry information within the central nervous system.

68. (E) Acetylcholine is one of the most well-understood neurotransmitters. It's important for learning and memory. In Alzheimer's disease, neurons that produce acetylcholine begin to deteriorate. Additionally, this neurotransmitter acts as a messenger at every junction between motor neurons, which carry information from the brain and spinal cord to the body's muscles.

69. (B) In Parkinson's disease, neurons that produce dopamine undergo cell death. This leads to a decrease in the body's supply of dopamine. Without dopamine, movement becomes difficult. As the disease progresses, dopamine levels drop further and symptoms worsen; patients develop tremors and have difficulty walking.

70. (B) GABA, or gamma-aminobutyric acid, is the primary inhibitory neurotransmitter in the body. When GABA levels become too low, seizures, tremors, and insomnia can occur.

71. (A) Agonists refer to any molecule that can bind to a receptor site and stimulate a response. Although we have our own naturally occurring neurotransmitters that bind and stimulate receptors in the brain, many drugs elicit their effect by hijacking our receptors and mimicking the effects of natural neurotransmitters. Antagonists are molecules that bind a receptor site and block its stimulation. Endorphins are the naturally occurring neurotransmitters that bind to the same receptors as opiates. The name comes from the combination of the words "endogenous" and "morphine."

72. (C) A synapse is the junction between the terminal axon tip of the sending neuron and the dendrite fiber of the receiving neuron. It is less than one-millionth of an inch wide.

Chapter 5: Sensation and Perception

73. (A) Selective attention is the focusing of conscious awareness on a specific stimulus. When in a crowded room with many conversations occurring, your mind will block out the stimulus from the surrounding conversations while it focuses on the voice of the person to whom you are talking.

74. (C) The minimum intensity of physical energy required to produce any sensation at all in a person is called absolute threshold. The difference threshold, also known as the just-noticeable difference, is the smallest change in stimulation that can be detected 50 percent of the time.

75. (B) Weber's law states that the JND (just-noticeable difference) for any given sense is a proportion of the stimulation being judged. Hearing, for example, is very sensitive: we can detect a 0.3 percent change in sound. By contrast, producing a JND in taste requires a 20-percent change.

76. (E) The transparent protective coating over the front part of the eye is the cornea. The lens focuses the light onto the retina. The iris is the colored part of the eye. The pupil is the small opening in the iris where light enters. The fovea is the area of the retina that is the center of the visual field.

77. (B) The lens is the transparent part of the eye inside the pupil that focuses light onto the retina.

78. (A) An afterimage is a visual sensation that continues after the original stimulus is removed. For example, if you stare at a blue square, you will see a yellow afterimage.

79. (C) On the basis of his work with afterimages, physiologist Ewald Hering suggested that the visual system codes colors by using two complementary pairs: red/green and blue/yellow. Hering's idea became known as the opponent-process theory. The trichromatic theory says there are three different kinds of cones in the retina, not related to an afterimage. The volley principle has to do with receptors in the ear and has no relation to an afterimage.

80. (B) Trichromats are people who have normal color vision. Trichromats perceive all hues by combining the colors red, blue, and green.

81. (B) Conduction hearing loss is a less common form of hearing loss. It occurs when the mechanical system that transfers sound waves from the inner ear to the outer ear becomes damaged.

82. (B) Transduction refers to the process in which a sense organ, in this case the nose, changes or transforms physical energy into electrical signals that become neural impulses, which may be sent to the brain for processing. Choice (A) is incorrect because adaptation refers to a decreased response to a stimulation. Choice (C) is incorrect because sensation is a meaningless bit of information. Choice (D) is incorrect because perception is meaningful sensory experiences.

83. (D) We can only be aware of a small amount of visual stimulus at any given time. Selective inattention can lead to inattentional blindness, the failure to see objects in your line of sight when your focus is directed somewhere else. In this case, your attention was so highly focused on the road in front of you that you failed to see the severe accident on the other side of the road while driving home.

84. (B) Loudness is our subjective experience of a sound's intensity. The brain calculates loudness from specific physical energy, in this case the amplitude of sound waves. Pitch is our subjective experience of a sound being high or low. The frequency of the sound wave is measured in cycles.

85. (D) The olfactory cells are located in two one-inch-square patches of tissue in the uppermost part of the nasal passages.

86. (A) Convergence is a binocular cue for depth perception based on signals sent from muscles that turn the eye. To focus on near or approaching objects, these muscles turn the eyes inward, toward the nose. Retinal disparity refers to the different position of the eyes receiving slightly different images. Shape constancy refers to the tendency to perceive an object as retaining the same shape even when you view it from different angles. Interposition comes into play when objects overlap.

87. (C) Size constancy refers to our tendency to perceive objects as remaining the same size even when their images on the retina are continually growing or shrinking. Choice (A), shape constancy, refers to changing shapes, not necessarily size.

88. (E) Convergence is a binocular cue, meaning the cue depends on the movement of both eyes. Choices (A), (B), (C), and (D) are monocular cues, that is, cues that are produced from a single eye.

89. (C) The cochlea is located in the inner ear. The cochlea contains the receptors for hearing, and its function is transduction, transforming vibrations into nerve impulses that are sent to the brain for processing into auditory information.

90. (B) The gate control theory explains that you may not notice pain from a headache or injury while thoroughly involved in some other activity, because impulses from that activity close the neural gate and block the passage of painful impulses.

91. (D) Rods are photoreceptors that contain a single chemical, called rhodopsin, which is activated by small amounts of light. Because rods are extremely light sensitive, they allow us to see in dim light, but to see only black, white, and shades of gray. Cones are photoreceptors that contain three chemicals called opsins, which are activated in bright light and allow us to see color.

92. 81. (A) In bottom-up processing, receptors register information about the external environment and send it up to the brain for analysis and interpretation. Bottom-up processing is initiated by stimulus input. An example of bottom-up processing is putting together a jigsaw puzzle (Friedrich, 2001). If you don't have the puzzle's original box with a picture of the finished product, you have to look at the shapes and colors of the pieces to determine how they fit together. That is essentially bottom-up processing.

93. (D) Top-down processing refers to the use of contextual information in pattern recognition. For example, understanding difficult handwriting is easier when reading complete sentences than when reading single and isolated words. This is because the meanings of the surrounding words provide a context to aid understanding.

94. (D) Sensory adaptation is the process in which changes in the sensitivity of sensory receptors occur in relation to the stimulus. All senses are believed to experience sensory adaptation. However, some experimental psychologists say that the sense of pain does not experience this phenomenon.

95. (E) In the context of light, the wavelength is the distance between the peak of one light wave to the peak of the next. Electromagnetic waves vary in size from nearly microscopic gamma rays to the long broadcast bands. Only a small fraction of specific wavelengths are part of the visible light spectrum. Therefore, wavelength determines whether light is visible. Of the visible spectrum of light, hue or color is also determined by the light's wavelength.

96. (D) David Hubel and Torsten Wiesel received the Nobel Prize for their work on feature detectors. These specialized nerve cells reside in the occipital lobe of the cerebral cortex. They receive information from individual ganglion cells in the retina. Feature detectors respond to specific features of visual input and pass the information along to other cortical areas.

97. (E) The frequency theory suggests that the brain reads pitch by interpreting the frequency of neural impulses traveling up the auditory nerve. This theory contrasts with Hermann von Helmholtz's place theory, which suggests that we hear different pitches because different sound waves trigger activity in different regions of the cochlea's basilar membrane.

98. (B) Our sense of taste represents a basic survival function that attracted our ancestors to sources of energy. We have five different types of taste receptors, and they each serve a unique purpose. A sweet taste indicates a readily available energy source, whereas a bitter taste represents the possible presence of a poisonous compound. For this reason, most young children are inherently unwilling to eat bitter-tasting vegetables, but they will usually begin to accept the bitter taste of many vegetables after repeated exposure.

Chapter 6: Consciousness, Sleep, and Dreams

99. (A) The automatic process is any activity that requires little awareness, takes minimal attention, and does not interfere with ongoing activities. All of these characteristics describe what sometimes happens while people are driving a familiar route. Choice (B) requires full awareness. Choices (C), (D), and (E) do not pertain to this question.

100. (B) The circadian rhythm refers to a biological clock that is genetically programmed to regulate physiological responses within a time period of 24–25 hours (one day). Most of us operate on a 24-hour day and thus set back our sleep-wake circadian clock about one hour each day. Choice (A), interval timing clock, works more like a stopwatch, which helps a person to time his or her movements, such as knowing when to start or stop an activity. Choice (C), biological clock, is an internal timing device used to regulate various physiological responses, but it is not genetically programmed.

101. (D) Melatonin is a hormone that is secreted by the pineal gland. Melatonin secretion increases with darkness and decreases with light, playing a role in the regulation of circadian rhythms and in promoting sleep. Serotonin is related to mood levels and mood control. Norepinephrine works as a stress hormone and is directly related to "fight or flight." Epinephrine, when produced by the body, increases heart rate and blood pressure. Dopamine also relates to the sympathetic nervous system, increasing heart rate and blood pressure.

102. (A) Non-REM stage 3 sleep is also called slow wave, or delta, sleep. It is characterized by waves of very high amplitude and low frequency, called delta waves.

103. (D) REM sleep is also known as paradoxical sleep. REM brain waves have fast frequency and low amplitude and look very similar to beta waves, which occur when you are wide-awake. During this stage your body is physiologically aroused, but your voluntary muscles are paralyzed. REM sleep stage is highly associated with dreaming.

104. (D) Sleepwalking and sleep talking occur during non-REM stage 3 sleep. Many people confuse this answer with the REM stage because of the belief that sleepwalkers and sleep talkers are acting out their dreams that occur in REM. But voluntary muscles are paralyzed during REM; therefore, people cannot physically act out their dreams. Because non-REM stage 3 sleep is the deepest stage of sleep, very often people do not remember sleepwalking or sleep talking.

105. (C) From infancy to adolescence, the total amount of time spent in sleep and the percentage spent in REM gradually decline. Newborns sleep about 17 hours a day, and 50 percent of that time is spent in REM. A four-year-old sleeps about 10 hours, and 25 percent of that time is spent in REM. From adolescence to old age, we maintain the same amount of sleep time, approximately 7.5 hours of sleep, and the same percentage of REM sleep, about 20 percent or less.

106. (B) Choice (B) defines the term *adaptive sleep theory*. Support for the adaptive theory comes from observations that large predatory animals sleep more and wherever they want, while smaller prey sleep less and in more protected areas. Choice (A) defines the term *repair theory*.

107. (C) The activation-synthesis theory of dreams says that dreaming represents the random and meaningless activity of nerve cells in the brain. Choices (A) and (B) represent the Freudian view of dreaming. Choice (E) represents the extension of waking life theory.

108. (E) Freud's view on dreaming was the belief that dreams protect the conscious from the realization of our unconscious desires and wishes, especially sexual or aggressive wishes. Our dreams transform these desires into harmless symbols and do not disturb our sleep. Extension of waking life is based on the belief that our dreams reflect the same thoughts and concerns we have when we are awake. The activation-synthesis theory suggests that dreams are a product of neural firings in our brain. The spiritual world theory states that dreams represent the time when one enters the spiritual world, which helps a person to reflect on the past, present, or future, through communication with the souls of people who are no longer with us.

109. (B) A person with sleep apnea may repeatedly stop breathing, momentarily wake up, resume breathing, and return to sleep. Narcolepsy is marked by excessive sleepiness usually in the form of sleep attacks. Insomnia refers to difficulties in either going to sleep or staying asleep through the night.

110. (A) Night terrors are frightening experiences that often start with screaming, followed by sudden waking in a fearful state with rapid breathing. They usually occur in stage 4 sleep. Night terrors are often confused with nightmares, which usually occur during REM sleep. They are also frightening, but usually produce clear anxiety-producing images.

111. (C) Narcolepsy is a chronic disorder. It is characterized by sleep attacks or short lapses of sleep throughout the day. These attacks are accompanied by REM sleep and muscle paralysis.

112. (B) REM sleep looks very similar to beta waves. Physiologically a person is aroused during this stage and muscles are paralyzed, which is why this stage is known as "paradoxical sleep." Choice (A) is incorrect because REM sleep is not the deepest stage of sleep; stage 4 is. Choice (C) is incorrect because body paralysis occurs during REM; therefore, a person cannot sleepwalk. Choice (D) is incorrect because night terrors occur in stage 4 sleep, not REM. Choice (E) is incorrect because a person's vital signs are actually very aroused in REM.

113. (B) A neurobiological theory of dreams, the reverse learning theory likens the process of dreaming to a computer in that it was "offline" during dreaming or the REM phase of sleep. One supporting fact for this hypothesis was brought about by recent studies in which it was found that if a person falls asleep soon after something bad or negative has happened, after waking up, everything will be remembered in detail, as if it happened a few minutes ago. Therefore, if there is a possibility of psychological trauma, it is best not to allow the victim to go to sleep for as long as possible because the absence of dreams will help erase unpleasant experiences from memory.

114. (A) One of the main reasons people daydream is to escape reality. It is usually done without effort or recognition. In choices (C), (D), and (E), a person does recognize he or she is doing something to escape, usually with more effort. Dreaming, on the other hand, occurs without any recognition.

115. (C) Insomnia is difficulty with either falling asleep or staying asleep. Narcolepsy is a disorder characterized by sleep attacks. Sleep apnea is marked by periods of sleep when a person stops breathing.

116. (E) Delta waves are slow waves with a very high amplitude and very low frequency. Delta waves are part of stage 4 sleep, not REM. All of the other choices are definite characteristics of REM sleep.

117. (C) An adult getting approximately seven to eight hours of sleep will go through four to five cycles of sleep. A full cycle begins with stage 1 sleep and ends with REM. The next cycle starts at stage 2 and goes up to stage 3 and 4 and back to REM again. Individuals do not return to stage 1 until around the time they are going to wake up.

118. (B) Each stage is 90 minutes. The first cycle includes stages 1, 2, 3, 4, and REM. The next cycle begins with stage 2.

119. (A) Many psychologists in the 1950s believed that if people were denied REM sleep and therefore could not dream, they would suffer mentally and emotionally. Studies today continue to show long-term detrimental behavioral problems when people do not get enough REM sleep. This is not the case with the other stages of sleep.

120. (C) Alpha waves are characteristic of this period before entering sleep. Delta waves are characteristic of stage 4 sleep. Beta waves are characteristics of REM sleep. Theta waves are characteristic of stage 1 sleep.

121. (D) The reticular formation arouses and alerts the forebrain. It is stimulated in sleeping animals. Choices (A) and (B) have to do with memory and emotion. Choice (E) has to do with breathing and heart rate.

122. (B) Extension of waking life theory suggests that dreams reflect our thoughts and concerns from our waking lives, or issues we have on our minds when we are awake. Freud's theory suggests our dreams represent our repressed desires and fantasies. Activation synthesis suggests dreams are a product of our neural firings in the brain. Spiritual world theory suggests when we dream we are in touch with those who have passed on.

123. (E) As an adult, 80 percent of our sleep is in NREM. In other words, adults spend 20 percent of their sleep in REM sleep.

124. (A) Beta waves are characteristic of REM sleep. REM sleep is where 90 percent of our dreaming occurs; therefore, beta waves are characteristic of a person who is dreaming.

125. (A) REM rebound is the idea that we go straight to REM sleep when we are sleep deprived.

Chapter 7: Drugs and Hypnosis

126. (A) Ernest Hilgard developed the hidden observer concept. The idea was that under a hypnotic trance a person's conscious is actually divided into two parts. The hypnotized part will feel little or no pain and will respond that way orally. The unhypnotized part will feel normal pain sensations but will not answer the question orally. This part can respond to the question by tapping one's fingers.

127. (D) While using drugs to fit in with peers is an unhealthy behavior, it does not indicate that someone suffers from a drug use disorder. A drug use disorder is characterized by impaired control, risky use, social impairment, and continued drug use despite adverse effects.

128. (C) The definition for dependency is a change in the nervous system that results in a person's needing the drug to prevent painful withdrawal symptoms. Choice (A) defines tolerance. Choice (B) defines addiction. Choice (D) defines withdrawal symptoms.

129. (B) When excited, neurons secrete neurotransmitters. After a brief period of time, the neurotransmitters are reabsorbed back into the neuron. This process is called reuptake. If reuptake did not occur, the neurotransmitter would remain in the synapse and neurons would be continually stimulated. Cocaine blocks reuptake, which leads to increased neural stimulation, causing increased physical and psychological arousal.

130. (E) Stimulants, by definition, increase activities of the central nervous system. This results in heightened alertness, arousal, and euphoria. Cocaine, caffeine, nicotine, and amphetamines are all stimulants. Heroin is an opiate, which is highly addictive and used for pain reduction.

131. (D) Tolerance occurs after a person uses a drug repeatedly over a period of time. The drug no longer produces the desired effects. Withdrawal is the painful symptoms that occur when a person is no longer taking an addictive drug. Addiction is the behavioral pattern marked by a compulsive desire for the drug.

132. (C) Heroin, similar to morphine and codeine, is an opiate. While some opiates are prescribed to relieve pain, heroin is used as a recreational drug for its euphoric effects. As with other opiates, frequent use of heroin leads to the development of drug tolerance and severe withdrawal symptoms that can begin within hours of the last use.

133. (A) Hallucinogens are a separate category from stimulants, eliminating choices (B) and (E). Choice (C) describes some characteristics of opiates. Hallucinogens are not depressants, thereby eliminating choice (D).

134. (A) The most important part of hypnosis is suggestibility. This eliminates choices (B), (C), and (E). Choice (D) is incorrect because hypnotists do not tell people they are going to enter a trance; instead their suggestions are much more subtle. Some examples would be a suggestion of feeling relaxed, feeling sleepy, or having a floating feeling.

135. (C) Alcohol is a depressant that slows the sympathetic nervous system. It reduces your self-awareness and self-control. Alcohol disrupts memory formation and can have long-term effects on cognition in heavy drinkers. People's alcohol consumption and behavior while drinking can be influenced by strongly held, socially reinforced beliefs about the drug, such as its ability to make socializing easier.

136. (C) Barbiturates are "downers," which means they slow down or depress the central nervous system, while amphetamines are often referred to as "uppers," which means they stimulate the central nervous system.

137. (B) This question is asking, in pretty general terms, the four major effects of psychoactive drugs. Appetite, sex drive, and digestion are too specific and therefore eliminate choices (A), (C), (D), and (E). Choice (B) gives the overall impacts of any psychoactive drugs.

138. (D) Heroin is an opiate. Opiates are generally used as painkillers. They do increase feelings of euphoria and are highly addictive. The other choices are all examples of depressants. Depressants slow down the central nervous system, decreasing anxiety and increasing relaxation.

139. (B) Marijuana is a hallucinogen, causing psychological effects. Marijuana is believed to act sometimes as a depressant because of its physiological effects, including relaxed inhibitions and feelings of euphoria. Choices (A), (C), (D), and (E) do not cause all of the symptoms listed in the question.

140. (E) Hypnosis is most commonly used to ease pain, stop unhealthy habits, and help patients recall memories. Hypnosis is not used for marriage counseling.

141. (E) Anton Mesmer believed a force called "animal magnetism" could pass into a patient's body, curing a variety of symptoms. The term *mesmerized*, meaning "spellbound or hypnotized," comes from Anton Mesmer.

142. (C) The key term in this question is *susceptible*. If a person is susceptible to hypnosis, it means he or she has more than likely entered into a hypnotic trance. While a person is under a trance, a hypnotist will suggest that the person does not feel pain. Someone who does not believe in, or has not entered into a hypnotic trance, will probably not report lower levels of pain.

143. **(E)** Posthypnotic exhortation is a made-up term. Posthypnotic amnesia is not remembering what happened during hypnosis. Hidden observer is the belief that your consciousness is divided into two parts while under a trance. Suggestibility is what allows people under hypnosis to perform a certain behavior. Hypnotic analgesia is the inability to feel pain while still conscious.

Chapter 8: Classical Conditioning

144. **(A)** The UCS, unconditioned stimulus, is a stimulus that automatically causes an organism to respond in a specific way. In this case the substance automatically makes the coyotes ill. The CS, or conditioned stimulus, is an originally neutral stimulus that is paired with an unconditioned stimulus and eventually produces the desired responses in an organism. In this case the sheep's wool was originally neutral and is now associated with the substance. The CR, or conditioned response, is the response an organism produces when only a conditioned stimulus is present. In this case the conditioned response is the aversion to the sheep, which occurred after conditioning made an association between the substance and the sheep.

145. **(C)** Generalization is the tendency for a stimulus that is similar to the original conditioned stimulus to elicit a response that is similar to the conditioned response. In this situation, the coyotes showed the same aversion response to the nearby sheep as they did to the original flock of sheep.

146. **(D)** This is a straightforward definition question. Choice (D) clearly defines the Premack Principle.

147. **(A)** *Variable interval* means "an unspecified amount of time." Pop quizzes are given after an unspecified amount of time. Choice (B) is incorrect because *ratio* refers to a specific number of times someone has to do something in order to be rewarded. In terms of pop quizzes a student cannot do anything to make a pop quiz happen any sooner or later; it is simply an interval of time. *Fixed ratio* requires a person to do something a certain number of specified times to be rewarded, for example, getting paid on commission. *Fixed interval* is a set amount of time between reinforcement, for example, a midterm exam.

148. **(B)** Extinction is the reduction in a response when the conditioned stimulus is no longer followed by the unconditioned stimulus. As a result, the conditioned stimulus tends to no longer elicit the conditioned response. In this case if the bell is no longer paired with the food, eventually the dogs will stop salivating at the sound of the bell.

149. **(D)** The unconditioned stimulus is some stimulus that triggers or elicits a physiological reflex, such as fear. In this case Little Albert automatically had a fear response after hearing the loud noise, which makes it the unconditioned stimulus.

150. (A) Because a stimulus must produce a response and not the other way around, choices (B), (C), and (E) can all be eliminated. Choice (D) is incorrect because a conditioned stimulus must produce a conditioned response. Conditioned stimulus means that the stimulus was formerly neutral; therefore, the response is elicited from the conditioned stimulus and called the conditioned response. That leaves choice (A). The UCS produces the UCR.

151. (B) The sailor's hat was a formerly neutral stimulus. Now Dylan has made an association between the sailor's hat and feeling nauseated. The sailor's hat is therefore the conditioned stimulus.

152. (D) Variable ratio is correct because when fishing, a person does not know when or how long it is going to take to catch a fish. Variable interval is incorrect because *interval* simply means "time." Although fishing does take time, you have to do something to catch a fish, such as putting the fishing line in the water.

153. (C) *Fixed ratio* applies to any job that works on commission. In this context, *ratio* means "the number of times you do something to get rewarded." *Fixed* means "a set number of times you do something to get rewarded." When people work on commission they know how much merchandise they have to sell in order to get paid.

154. (A) The UCS is a stimulus that triggers or elicits a physiological reflex. In this case, it is the job interview, because it automatically made him nervous. The UCR is unlearned and innate. In this case feeling anxious is a direct, involuntary response to the job interview. The CS is a formerly neutral stimulus. In this case prior to the job interview, the passenger was never afraid to fly. The CR is elicited from the CS; in this case, feeling anxious and nervous about flying would be the CR.

155. (B) Prior to the injection of the drug that weakens mice's immune systems, the saccharine-flavored water had no effect. Once paired with the injection, the saccharine-flavored water had the same effect.

156. (D) The unconditioned response for this advertisement is the desire to buy the food product after seeing the cartoon character associated with the food product long enough that the mere sight of the food product will elicit a response to buy it*.

---

*Kelly, Bridget, Libby Hattersley, Lesley King, and Victoria Flood. Persuasive Food Marketing to Children: Use of Cartoons and Competitions in Australian Commercial Television Advertisements. *Health Promotion International* 23 (no. 4): 337–344. https://academic.oup.com/heapro/article/23/4/337/628113

Rose, Gregory M., Altaf Merchant, and Aysen Bakir. "Fantasy in Food Advertising Targeted at Children." *Journal of Advertising* 41, no. 3 (2012), 75-90, DOI: 10.2753/JOA0091-3367410305 https://www.tandfonline.com/doi/abs/10.2753/JOA0091-3367410305

157. (B) Because the unconditioned stimulus is a stimulus that elicits an involuntary response, the advertisers intentionally placed cartoon characters in their ads knowing that that would elicit a desire to buy food products.

158. (C) Choice (C) is the definition of *classical conditioning*. The other choices do not include the formerly neutral stimulus, which is what classical conditioning is all about.

159. (A) Until paired with the food, the bell did not elicit a response of salivation. Therefore, the bell is the CS. The food automatically made the dogs salivate; therefore, it is the UCS.

160. (E) Choice (E) is the definition of *desensitization therapy*. Choice (D) sounds like it could also be the correct choice, but desensitization therapy does not use the concept of generalization.

161. (C) Because classical conditioning has to do with a stimulus and response, choice (C) has to be the correct answer. Choice (A) has to do with operant conditioning. Choices (B), (D), and (E) all have to do with social cognitive learning.

162. (D) Choice (D) is the only one that has to do with learned behavior. Choices (A) and (B) are both related to natural physiological occurrences in the body. Choices (C) and (E) are both related to innate behavior.

163. (B) Choice (B) uses the term *unconditioned association*, which is directly related to classical conditioning. The other choices do not specifically discuss a stimulus and a response.

Chapter 9: Operant Conditioning and Cognitive Learning

164. (A) A token economy is a system of behavior modification based on the systematic reinforcement of target behavior. The reinforcers are symbols or "tokens" that can be exchanged for other reinforcers.

165. (B) Primary reinforcers are biological. Food, drink, and pleasure are the most common examples of primary reinforcers. Most human reinforcers are secondary, or conditioned. Examples include money, grades in schools, and tokens. Secondary reinforcers acquire their power via a history of association with primary reinforcers or other secondary reinforcers. For example, if dollars were no longer going to be used as money, then dollars would lose their power as a secondary reinforcer.

166. (A) Operant conditioning is a kind of learning in which a behavior is performed, followed by a consequence. Learning takes place as a result of some voluntary action by the learner. In classical conditioning, learning takes place without choice. The stimulus causes the response. Choice (B) is incorrect because it is actually the opposite. Operant conditioning takes place after the response, while classical conditioning takes place before the response. Choice (C) is also the opposite. Classical conditioning is learning by association, and operant conditioning is learning by reinforcement. Choices (D) and (E) are completely incorrect. Classical conditioning is not part of social cognitive learning.

167. (C) Very often students get confused between negative reinforcement and punishment. Negative reinforcement occurs when something unpleasant is taken away if the subject does something. It is conditional. Punishment is not the same as negative reinforcement. It is an attempt to weaken a response, or a behavior, by following it with something unpleasant. It is not conditional. Because the basketball player should not commit flagrant fouls, he was suspended; therefore, it is a punishment.

168. (D) The law of effect says that if a random act is followed by a pleasurable consequence, such actions are strengthened and will likely occur again. Choice (D) is the definition of the *law of effect*.

169. (E) Shaping is a procedure in which the experimenter successively reinforces behaviors that lead up to the desired behavior. Many students get confused between shaping and chaining. Chaining is an instructional procedure that involves reinforcing responses in a sequence to form a more complex behavior. In terms of the Skinner box, B. F. Skinner used shaping to condition his rats to press the lever.

170. (B) Variable interval refers to an unknown amount of time, more or less waiting for a desired response to occur. Because it does not matter how many times you check social media, the correct answer is variable interval and not variable ratio. Ratio refers to the number of desired acts required before reinforcement will occur.

171. (B) Positive reinforcement occurs when something the subject wants is added to encourage the wanted behavior to continue. Negative reinforcement occurs when something unpleasant is taken away once the wanted behavior continues. Both have the same goal, to repeat wanted behavior.

172. (B) Choice (B) is the definition of *latent learning*. Often humans and animals need motivation or good reason to show their behavior, which does not mean they have not learned the behavior. Choice (A) can apply to almost any form of learning. Choice (D) defines operant conditioning. Choice (E) can sound similar, but latent learning does not say the actual learning occurs after the behavior, just the demonstration of the learning.

173. (C) Edward Tolman's theory of latent learning suggested that the concept of response needed to include a range of behaviors that would allow learners to reach their goals. Tolman felt that learning usually occurs before the goal is reached.

174. (D) A cognitive map is a learned mental image of a spatial environment. This image is usually learned without the learner realizing he or she has learned it. Choice (D) is the only answer that suggests this.

175. (A) Insight is learning that occurs rapidly based on understanding all the elements of a problem. In this case, the chimps learned how to obtain the banana shortly after figuring out their environment.

176. (E) A learning set is the ability to become increasingly more effective in solving problems the more practice you have. In this case the monkeys learned how to choose the correct box based on their problem-solving techniques used with each trial. Based on this idea, *learning sets* really means learning how to learn.

177. (B) Social cognitive learning emphasizes the ability to learn by observation without firsthand experience. It does not specify that a person must observe rewarded behavior. Choice (D) can be confused for the correct answer, but it is too vague when the question is asking which statement best exemplifies social cognitive learning.

178. (A) In the Albert Bandura "bobo" doll experiment, the children who watched the video in which a person was rewarded for acting violently toward the doll were first to act aggressively. Although after being offered candy by the experimenter, children from all of the groups did demonstrate aggressive behavior, initially it was the model-reward condition.

179. (C) Vicarious learning, or observational learning, is simply learning by observing other people, as Devyn did in this scenario.

180. (B) Insight learning occurs rapidly as a result of understanding all of the elements of a problem. In this case, Spencer suddenly arrived at the answer after working out the elements of the math problem. Choice (A) refers to learning that is not immediately reflected in the behavior. Choice (C) is simply learning how to learn. Choice (D) is vague and incorrect. Choice (E) is learning based on reward and punishment.

181. (D) Learned helplessness is defined as failure to take steps to avoid or escape from an aversive stimulus that occurs as a result of previous unavoidable painful stimuli. The dogs, having no way out for several minutes, gave up, even when there was a viable escape.

182. (B) Spontaneous recovery is the reappearance of an extinguished response after some time has passed. In this case, Jada's fear of going to the dentist returned only when she had to go back for a root canal. That is an example of spontaneous recovery. Generalization would have been if Jada feared all doctors as a result of her fear of the dentist.

Chapter 10: Memory

183. **(C)** Encoding is the process of transferring information from short-term memory to long-term memory by paying attention to it or by forming new associations. In this case Katie made a new association with the number 111. Choice (D) does seem like it could be the correct answer because it is the ability to retain information; however, encoding gives a more specific explanation.

184. **(A)** Episodic memory is a type of memory that involves knowledge of a specific event or personal experience. In this case, remembering that you got a bicycle is a personal memory. Choices (B), (D), and (E) are all examples of semantic memory. Choice (C) is an example of procedural memory.

185. **(C)** Procedural memory is a type of implicit or unconscious memory. Procedural memory helps us perform specific tasks without conscious awareness of previous experiences. In this case, Sophia can perform the task of riding a bike even though she cannot remember the specific experience of learning to ride a bike.

186. **(D)** The hippocampus transfers words, facts, and personal events from short-term memory to long-term memory. People with damage to the hippocampus cannot save any declarative memories. Choice (C) could be tempting, but the amygdala deals with emotional feelings associated with memories, not the transfer from STM to LTM.

187. **(B)** Echoic memory is a form of sensory memory that holds auditory information for one to two seconds. In this case you are able to recall your friend's exact words because they are still in your echoic memory. Iconic memory is a form of sensory memory that holds visual information for a brief period of time. Sensory memory is the initial process that receives and holds environmental information. Short-term memory is the process of holding information for a short period of time, but it is not what would have been used in this particular situation.

188. **(E)** For information to be processed it must go through three steps: Encoding using sensory receptors is the initial step because it is picking up information from the environment in its raw form. Storing information is the second step in the process; to retrieve the information at a later time, the information has to be stored properly to begin with. The third step is the ability, when necessary, to retrieve it. Information cannot be retrieved before it has been stored.

189. **(E)** The only false statement is choice (E). Procedural memory involves skills, habits, and things learned through classical conditioning, not declarative memory. Declarative memory involves facts or events such as scenes, stories, words, or conversations.

190. (D) State-dependent learning is the idea that we recall information more easily when we are in the same physiological or emotional state as when the information was originally encoded. In this case when Jeff drank alcohol, it put him in the same physiological state, enabling him to remember the details of the crime.

191. (B) Short-term memory is called working memory because it can hold only a limited amount of information for a short period of time, between 2 and 30 seconds. If during that time you become more involved in the information, it can last longer.

192. (C) Eidetic memory or imagery is the ability to examine a picture and then retain the detailed visual image. This is found in a small percentage of children. Flashbulb memories are vivid recollections of dramatic incidents. Semantic memories are declarative memories consisting of factual knowledge. Echoic memories hold auditory information. Iconic memories hold visual images.

193. (A) The amygdala is responsible for emotionally charged memories.

194. (B) Choice (B) specifically describes the phenomenon behind the primacy effect. Words at the beginning of a list are more likely to be remembered because of proper rehearsal and encoding techniques. Choices (C) and (E) would apply to the recency effect.

195. (D) Semantic memory involves knowledge of facts, concepts, words, definitions, and language rules. Episodic memory is incorrect because it involves specific personal experiences. Procedural memory is incorrect because it involves memories of skills and habits.

196. (A) Long-term memory does have an unlimited capacity. Short-term memory can hold an average of seven items for up to 30 seconds. The other choices were simply put there to confuse the reader.

197. (B) Choice (B) is the definition of *maintenance rehearsal*. Intentionally repeating information can help the information remain in your short-term memory for a longer period of time.

198. (A) Short-term memory is also called working memory for this very reason. Because it only has a limited amount of space, one must make a conscious effort to keep the information there for a short period of time before it disappears. The other choices do not apply to the scenario.

199. (D) Chunking is combining separate items of information into a larger unit, then remembering chunks of information rather than individual items. Elaborate rehearsal involves actively making meaningful associations between information, not what was done in the scenario presented in the question. Maintenance rehearsal is simply repeating information.

200. (B) Making associations increases the likelihood that the information will be encoded properly. Repetition by itself does not ensure efficient encoding from STM to LTM.

201. (C) Maintenance rehearsal, the practice of intentionally repeating information, is necessary for information to remain in STM for up to 30 seconds. For information to be processed into LTM, elaborate rehearsal is necessary. Elaborate rehearsal involves making meaningful associations between information to be learned and information already stored in long-term memory.

202. (D) Chunking is the only choice that is not part of effortful encoding. Effortful encoding involves the transfer of information from STM to LTM either by repeating the information, rehearsing it, or making associations between new and old information.

Chapter 11: Remembering and Forgetting

203. (B) Eyewitness testimony refers to recalling or recognizing a suspect observed during a potentially disrupting emotional situation. Because of the concern of eyewitness testimony, studies have been conducted to show that people can be misled, especially if given false information. Furthermore, asking a person misleading questions can create false memories.

204. (C) This is a simple definition answer. Nodes are memory files. Schemas are not memory files but mental categories, which is why choice (E) can be confusing.

205. (D) The forgetting curve measures the amount of previously learned information that the subject can recall or recognize over time. Ebbinghaus himself forgot the greatest number of nonsense syllables within the first hour.

206. (B) Proactive interference occurs when old information, in this case the Spanish language, blocks or disrupts the remembering of related new information, in this case, the Italian language. Choice (A) is not correct because retroactive interference occurs when new information blocks the retrieval of old information learned earlier. Choices (C) and (D) refer to a type of amnesia that occurs after a head trauma.

207. (C) Retrograde amnesia involves memory loss for events that occurred before the time of the head trauma.

208. (E) Suppression is the process of deliberately trying to stop thinking about something. Repression is the unconscious process of forgetting past memories. Amnesia is usually brought on by some type of head trauma. Forgetting is the inability to retrieve, recall, or recognize information.

209. (B) Anterograde amnesia is the type of amnesia that prevents an individual from making new memories after a head trauma. Retrograde amnesia is the inability to recall events preceding a head trauma. Choices (C) and (D) refer to blocking or disrupting information.

210. (C) The method of loci is an encoding technique that creates visual associations between already memorized places and new items to be memorized. It is a three-step process that involves memorizing familiar places, creating associations for each item to be memorized, and putting each item into the memorized place. An example of this could be selecting a specific place in your apartment to keep your keys and always remembering that place. Based on this definition, choice (C) is the correct answer.

211. (D) The hippocampus works similar to the save button on your computer. It transfers a file into permanent storage on your hard drive. People with damage to the hippocampus cannot save any declarative memories, such as new words or personal events.

212. (C) The forgetting curve illustrates the results of Ebbinghaus's memory decay experiment in which he plotted the percentage of lists retained while relearning on the *y*-axis and the time in days since initial learning on the *x*-axis. He found that newly learned information fades quickly, then levels off with more time.

213. (B) Remember, retrograde interference is when new information disrupts the retrieval of old information. In this case Ava studied the bones in the foot, the new information, which interfered with remembering the bones in the hand, the old information. Choice (A) is an example of proactive interference.

214. (D) Implicit memory is information that either was unintentionally committed to memory or was unintentionally retrieved from memory. In this case, Jack did not realize he remembered where a particular piece of information was on a page; therefore, it is an example of implicit memory. Explicit memory is intentionally committing information to memory.

215. (B) Recognition involves identifying previously learned information with the help of more external cues. A multiple-choice test is an example of recognition. Choice (A) is an example of recall, not recognition. Choice (D) was placed there to confuse students. Recognition is not creating entirely new responses.

216. (D) Recall involves retrieving previously learned information, in this case, items from the grocery store, without the aid of or with very few external cues.

217. (A) The method of loci creates a visual association between already memorized places and new items to be memorized. In this scenario, the playroom is the "already memorized place." The toys are the "to be memorized items." The peg method refers to an encoding process that creates associations between number-word rhymes and items to be memorized, for example, "one is thumb, two is shoe."

218. (B) Hermann Ebbinghaus's research showed that the greatest number of nonsense syllables were forgotten within the first hour. Afterward the amount of information forgotten levels off.

219. (A) Choice (A) is the definition of the *forgetting curve*.

220. (C) Recognition involves identifying previously learned information with the help of external cues. Multiple-choice questions exemplify recognition because cues exist. Recall involves retrieving previously learned information without the aid of external cues. A fill-in-the-blank test does not give the reader any cues to work with.

221. (A) Repression is a mental process that involves automatically hiding emotionally threatening or anxiety-provoking information in the unconscious. In this scenario, Kimberly did something embarrassing and her unconscious is blocking her memory of the event.

Chapter 12: Intelligence and Testing

222. (E) The Flynn effect is the substantial and long-sustained increase in both fluid and crystallized intelligence test scores measured in many parts of the world from roughly 1930 to the present day. Piaget believed that one's childhood plays a vital and active role in a person's development. Vygotsky believed children's thinking is affected by their knowledge of the social community (which is learnt from either technical or psychological cultural tools).

223. (B) Validity means the test is measuring what it is supposed to. A test with little or no validity produces results that could be produced by guessing or by chance. Choice (A) might confuse some students. A reliable test refers to the consistency: a person's score on a test at one point in time should be similar to the score obtained by the same person on a similar test at another point in time. Choice (D) refers to the test conditions, which should remain constant for all students taking the exam.

224. (D) Aptitude is the capacity to learn. Aptitude tests attempt to predict a person's ability to learn a new skill. IQ tests evaluate a person's intelligence quotient, which is his or her mental age divided by chronological age multiplied by 100. An achievement test measures what a person has already learned. An intelligence test specifically measures intelligence. Intelligence and aptitude tend to correlate.

225. **(D)** The calculation for the intelligence quotient is MA/CA × 100. In this case the MA is 5 and the CA is 4: 5/4 = 1.25; 1.25 × 100 = 125.

226. **(A)** The most widely used IQ tests are the Wechsler Adult Intelligence Scale for ages 16 and older and the Wechsler Intelligence Scale for Children for ages 3 to 16. The test includes a verbal and a performance section. The performance section contains a subtest that involves arranging pictures and assembling objects. The test was designed to eliminate any cultural biases by using nontraditional methods of testing.

227. **(C)** Spearman's two-factor theory says that intelligence has a general mental ability, which represents what different cognitive tasks have in common, as well as specific factors, which include mathematical and verbal skills.

228. **(E)** Sternberg's triarchic theory says that intelligence can be divided into three ways of gathering information: (1) Analytical thinking skills are measured by traditional intelligence tests. (2) Problem-solving skills require creative thinking and learning from experience. (3) Practical thinking skills help a person adjust and cope with his or her environment.

229. **(B)** Crystallized intelligence is the ability to retain information, while fluid intelligence refers to the ability to solve problems.

230. **(B)** Aptitude measures the capacity of the test taker to perform some task in the future. Choice (A) could look like the correct answer, but achievement measures an individual's knowledge of a particular subject.

231. **(C)** Savants are individuals, not necessarily children, with serious cognitive limitations such as mental retardation or autism who possess a remarkable talent in art or music. This eliminates choices (A), (B), (D), and (E).

232. **(E)** Charles Spearman's concept of "g," or general intelligence, is a unitary reference to a sort of overall smartness, which does not suggest the existence of more than one kind of intelligence.

233. **(A)** This is a definition question. An IQ of 55–70 represents a mild intellectual disability, 40–55 is a moderate intellectual disability, 25–40 is a severe intellectual disability, and below 25 is a profound intellectual disability.

234. (B) David Wechsler created both tests to eliminate cultural biases that exist in IQ testing by adding a performance component to his test. WAIS stands for the Wechsler Adult Intelligence Scale, and the WISC is the Wechsler Intelligence Scale for Children.

235. (D) The MMPI was originally designed to diagnose mental disorders, and it is still widely used as an assessment tool among clinicians. It has more than 500 true-or-false items designed to identify characteristics of personality and behavior.

236. (A) Choices (B), (C), and (D) can all be eliminated because Binet did not come up with the intelligence quotient; Lewis Terman did. Choice (E) is incorrect because Binet did not become the father of intelligence by discussing heritability.

237. (D) Studies have shown just how important environment can be to IQ scores, eliminating choices (A), (B), and (E). Data also show that an IQ can change by 10 to 15 points.

238. (B) Reaction range indicates the extent to which certain factors or abilities increase or decrease as a result of the environment. Although choice (C) may sound correct, reaction range does not say intelligence is completely due to environmental factors.

239. (A) In terms of genetics, fraternal twins are no different from other siblings—unlike identical twins, who share the same genetic material.

240. (C) Intelligence is a heritable trait. It is estimated that between 50 and 80 percent of intelligence test score variation can be attributed to genetic variation. However, the environment also plays a role in shaping a person's intelligence. Therefore, the pair that share the least genetic material and were raised in different environments will have the strongest negative correlation for intelligence. Adopted children and their adopted parents do not share significant genetic material (in comparison to identical twins, who are genetically identical) and were also raised in different environments.

241. (D) Sternberg's theory of three intelligences included analytical or academic problem-solving intelligence, which is assessed by traditional intelligence tests; creative intelligence, which involved reacting adaptively to new situations and generating novel ideas; and practical intelligence, which depends on the ability to astutely manage everyday tasks as well as other people.

Chapter 13: Thought and Language

242. (C) The prototype theory says that a person forms a concept by creating a mental image that is based on the average characteristics of an object. To identify new objects the person matches it to the one for which he or she has already formed a prototype. In this case a poodle has four legs, is average size, and has a nose, tail, and ears. Therefore he would be a prototype.

243. (D) Functional fixedness refers to a mental set that is characterized by the inability to see an object as having a function different from its usual one.

244. (A) An algorithm is a fixed set of rules that, if followed correctly, will eventually lead to a solution. Because this holds true for chess or checkers, (A) is the correct answer. A heuristic is a shortcut, allowing one to solve a problem more easily. A concept is a way to group objects. A prototype is the average characteristic of an object. Morphemes are the smallest meaningful combination of sounds.

245. (B) Availability heuristic says that we rely on information that is most prominent or easily recalled and overlook other information that is available but less prominent. In this case, students might choose (A), representative heuristic, but representative heuristic is similar to a stereotype, not prominent information.

246. (C) Convergent thinkers begin with a problem and come up with a single correct answer, while divergent thinkers begin with a problem and come up with many different solutions. Because an algorithm is a fixed set of rules, it is more likely used among convergent thinkers.

247. (D) Representative heuristic is problem solving based on stereotyping. In this case, Janet was stereotyping pilots by assuming the pilot was a male. Confirmation bias is incorrect because it means ignoring all information that does not support your beliefs. Janet was not ignoring anything; instead she was assuming. Convergent thinking is incorrect because Janet is not coming up with one solution to solve her problem. Availability heuristic is incorrect because Janet is not basing her answer on the most prominent information.

248. (B) Phonemes are the basic sounds of consonants and vowels.

249. (E) Noam Chomsky's theory states that all languages share a universal grammar and that all children inherit a mental program to learn this universal grammar.

250. (B) A schema is a conceptual framework that makes organizing and interpreting information easier. For example, a young child develops a schema for a dog. In the child's mind, dogs are furry and have four legs and a tail. The first time the child sees a cat, the child may mistakenly call her a dog. Once corrected, the child will update his or her existing schema for dogs and create a new schema for cats.

251. (C) Choice (C) is the only choice that states language development is innate. The other choices all support the Sapir-Whorf linguistic relativity hypothesis, which states that culture has a direct influence on determining the words that become part of our language.

252. (D) Confirmation bias is the tendency to find information that supports one's beliefs and ignore information that refutes them. This can sometimes prevent problem solving.

253. (B) Emotion-focused coping is a type of coping strategy. Coping strategies help to alleviate stress using emotional, cognitive, or behavioral methods. Emotion-focused coping attempts to alleviate stress by ignoring the stressor and giving attention to emotional needs related to one's stress reaction. People tend to resort to emotion-focused coping when they feel they have little control over the situation that causes them stress.

254. (A) Overregularization is when children apply grammatical rules without making appropriate exceptions. In this case "I goed to the store" indicates the use of the general rule that we form the past tense by adding "-ed" to the word.

255. (D) Noam Chomsky believes that children are born with a language acquisition device, an internal mechanism for processing speech, wired into the human brain.

256. (D) The one-word stage begins between the ages of 1 and 2 years old. In this stage of speech, young children begin to use sounds to communicate meaning.

257. (A) Framing refers to the way an issue is stated. How an issue is framed can affect a person's perception or decision. In this case women were more likely to go get a mammogram after hearing they could die if they didn't, rather than that it could save their life.

258. (B) This is the definition of the term *babbling*.

259. (A) Language stages refer to four different forms: phonemes, morphemes, syntax, and semantics. Easier to understand are the four stages: babbling, one-word phrase, two-word combinations, and sentences.

260. (E) A schema is a concept or cognitive framework that helps us organize and interpret information. In this case, Tina built a schema to represent the concept of a horse after seeing many pictures of horses. When Tina saw a cow for the first time, she tried to assimilate the animal into her existing schema for horses. With the experience of seeing both a cow and a horse, Tina was able to accommodate her schema for large, four-legged farm animals so that she can now distinguish between a cow and a horse.

261. (C) Availability heuristic is a general rule by which we rely on information that is more prominent and easily recalled and overlook other information that is less prominent. In this case, Steven knows most of the kids at his school but knows far fewer kids at the other school.

262. (C) Information retrieval is a problem-solving strategy that requires only the recovery of information from long-term memory. In this scenario, information retrieval is an important option when a solution must be found quickly. This is why choice (A), remembering a 16th birthday, is not the correct answer.

263. (E) Solving an anagram by trying every possible letter guarantees a solution. Therefore, this is an example of an algorithm.

264. (A) Functional fixedness is not a problem-solving strategy. It is a mental set characterized by the inability to see an object having multiple uses, different from its usual one.

265. (B) This is a definition question. Subgoals involve creating separate parts. Brainstorming involves coming up with various solutions, heuristics are shortcuts to problem solving, and algorithms are fixed sets of rules.

Chapter 14: Motivation

266. (D) Transcendent sex is the notion that the activation of primal psychological complexes sets up a transcendent episode, such as a feeling of well-being, which goes beyond sensual pleasure, and is caused by a change of consciousness. This idea is discussed in a popular book by Jenny Wade, a developmental psychologist.

267. (B) Choice (B) is the definition of *motivation*. The other choices do not correctly define motivation. Choice (A) defines fixed action pattern. Choice (C) defines a need. Choice (D) defines homeostasis. Choice (E) defines incentives.

268. (C) Instincts are innate tendencies or biological forces. The examples given are all innate feelings. Many students might look at choice (B) as the correct answer; however, emotions include subjective feelings. Instincts occur without subjectivity.

269. (D) The drive reduction theory says that a need results in a drive, creating a state of tension. A person must act to reduce that state of tension and return to homeostasis.

270. (C) A fixed action pattern is an innate biological force that predisposes an organism to behave in a fixed way in a specific environmental condition. In this case, the baboon is innately reacting to a condition in his environment, for survival. Choices (A) and (B) refer to needs. Needs are not innate patterns of behavior. Choices (D) and (E) are examples of conditioning.

271. (A) Intrinsic motivation involves behaviors that are personally rewarding and help us fulfill our beliefs. The other choices are examples of extrinsic motivation and positive reinforcement.

272. (C) According to Maslow's hierarchy of needs, level 3 is love and belonging. Level 3 represents the need to feel love, belonging, and affection from family, friends, and romantic partners.

273. (E) According to Maslow's hierarchy of needs, level 5 is self-actualization. Self-actualization is the fulfillment of one's unique potential. This involves developing and reaching our full potential as a unique individual.

274. (B) Esteem needs refer to achievement competency and gaining approval. In this case, earning a master's degree would be an example of achievement.

275. (B) The lateral hypothalamus regulates hunger by creating feelings of being hungry. The other choices are all examples of satiety signals.

276. (B) Choice (B) is the definition of *homeostasis*. Once a need is satisfied, the body will return to a state of equilibrium.

277. (D) The ventromedial hypothalamus regulates hunger by creating a feeling of satiety. Therefore, if the ventromedial hypothalamus is destroyed, the feeling of satiety will go away, causing the organism to overeat.

278. (E) Set point is a certain level of body fat our bodies try to maintain throughout our lives. When an individual's set point is high, so is his or her fat storage and body fat.

279. (A) The metabolic rate refers to how efficiently our body breaks down food into energy and how quickly our bodies burn it off. If a person has a low metabolic rate he or she will burn less fuel and store more fuel as fat, thus having a fatter body.

280. (E) Nutrition is the only choice that does not involve psychology. To put it another way, choices (A), (B), (C), and (D) all deal with issues other than physiological changes in the body.

281. (C) Gender identity differs from gender role in that gender identity is a subjective feeling about being male or female. Gender roles are stereotypical attitudes society designates as feminine or masculine.

282. (B) Gender roles are traditional attitudes society designates to both females and males. By age five, for example, boys learn stereotypical male behavior like playing sports. Girls learn the importance of physical appearance.

283. (B) The lateral hypothalamus signals hunger, while the ventromedial hypothalamus signals satiety.

284. (D) Maslow's hierarchy of needs demonstrates the importance of the order in which you satisfy your biological and social needs. Biological needs must be met first. If you are starving and homeless, you cannot worry about earning a master's degree.

285. (B) The incentive theory refers to environmental factors, such as external stimuli, reinforcers, or rewards that motivate a person to behave in a certain way. In this case the journalist was looking for recognition and the ability to increase his or her salary, both incentives based on external stimuli.

286. (C) Motivational behavior starts with a biological state in which an organism lacks something essential in its life. The need produces a drive, which in turn motivates action.

287. (A) Theory X is an authoritarian style that reflects an underlying belief that management must counteract an inherent human tendency to avoid work. Theory Y emphasizes a participative management style that motivates employees by fostering commitment to organizational objectives as opposed to a direct rewards or punishments approach. In other words, X theory managers believe employees will work for reward (benefits) or if threatened by punishment while Y theory managers believe employees are internally motivated to do good work.

288. (A) Based on extensive interviews of 18,000 people, Kinsey positioned people on the seven-point scale in which a rating of 0 meant that the person was "exclusively heterosexual" and a rating of 6 meant that a person was "exclusively homosexual." The main thrust of the scale was that, when looking at the deepest fantasies and admissions of sexual adults, human attraction rarely ran along straight lines of homosexual or heterosexual and that sexual behavior was enormously varied.

Chapter 15: Emotion

289. (B) Because the James-Lange theory focuses on the interpretation of physiological changes in the body, only choice (A) or (B) can be the correct answer. In this case, choice (B) is correct because in order to feel an emotion, according to the James-Lange theory, one must interpret the physiological change first before having the emotion.

290. (A) The two-factor theory states that emotions have two parts, physical arousal and cognitive appraisal. Jim and June experienced the same event; however, their resulting states of physical arousal and cognitive appraisal were quite different due to how they experienced the crash. June witnessed the accident from afar, while Jim was in very close proximity when the accident occurred. As a result, their emotional reactions to the same event were also quite different.

291. **(C)** James and Lange believed that our interpretation of our physiological changes in the body determines the emotions we are feeling. The problem with this theory is that many different emotions share the same physiological changes in the body. Therefore, physiological changes are not specific enough to determine emotions.

292. **(D)** Schachter and Singer conducted an experiment in which subjects were injected with adrenaline, causing increased heart rate and blood pressure. Half the subjects were placed in a room with an extremely happy person and the other half were placed in a room with an extremely angry person. Those in the room with the happy person associated their physiological changes with that person. Those in the room with the angry person associated their physiological changes with that person. These results helped to prove the Schachter-Singer theory, that perception is everything.

293. **(A)** Choice (A) is the only one that is based on a person's interpretation or perception of the situation before feeling an emotion.

294. **(D)** According to the facial feedback theory, our facial expressions can inform our emotions. When James Laird asked student participants to make a frowning expression in the guise of helping researchers attach electrodes to their faces, the students reported feeling slightly angry. Laird found similar results with other emotions.

295. **(A)** Ekman and Friesen's 1971 study found there were no significant differences between cultures when determining emotion from facial expressions. Regardless of cultural background, people are universally able to decipher facial expressions for basic emotions such as happiness, surprise, sadness, and anger.

296. **(C)** According to the Yerkes-Dodson law, performance on a task depends on the level of physiological arousal and the difficulty of the task. Low arousal is better for success on a difficult task. High arousal can help on the performance of easy tasks.

297. **(D)** Studies have shown that an individual's happiness is based more on positive feelings and overall life satisfaction than on the amount of money one makes.

298. **(A)** The adaptation level theory states that a person can quickly become comfortable receiving a large fortune and begin to take it for granted. Eventually this contributes less to long-term levels of happiness. The Yerkes-Dodson law has to do with physiological arousal and difficulty of task. The relative deprivation theory has to do with a sense of entitlement for others.

299. (E) The cognitive-appraisal theory assumes that your appraisal of a situation is often the primary cause of emotion. Choice (A), the affective-primacy theory, focuses on emotion before interpretation. Choices (B), (C), and (D) all focus on how physiological change influences our interpretation, not subjective feelings.

300. (B) Schachter and Singer believed that thoughts are important in establishing an emotional feeling. Based on the scenario, this belief would hold true and actually goes against the ideas behind the other choices.

301. (C) Cannon and Bard believed that physiological changes and the brain's interpretation happen at the same time. Although the James-Lange theory stated physiological changes happen first, Cannon and Bard believed that it is not one before the other. Instead, they occur at the same time.

302. (A) The cognitive-appraisal theory is the only one of these choices that focuses on subjectivity of an emotional experience based on the situation.

303. (B) The James-Lange theory said that physiological changes in the body determine the interpretation of an emotion. Therefore, we cry and then we know we are sad. The Cannon-Bard theory stated that those two occurrences happen simultaneously. The facial feedback theory focuses on facial muscle movement.

304. (B) Approach-avoidance conflict is a conflict that has one positive consequence and one negative consequence, unlike approach-approach conflict, which has two positive consequences.

305. (C) Because Latoya must choose between two excellent colleges, it has two positive consequences.

306. (D) The limbic system controls a large amount of our emotional stability.

307. (C) The opponent-process theory of emotion states that eventually our level of emotion changes with experience.

308. (E) Robert Zajonc believed that feelings or emotions might occur before thinking. This thinking is part of the affective-primacy theory. Choices (B), (C), and (D) all agree that interpretation occurs before the emotion.

309. (A) The hypothalamus deals with feeling and having emotional responses. The thalamus is the brain's "switchboard." The temporal lobe deals with auditory control. The parietal lobe deals with the sensation of touch. The amygdala controls emotional memories.

310. (A) The adaptation level theory states that we quickly become accustomed to receiving a new fortune and eventually take it for granted. This is why choice (A) is the correct answer. The other choices do not refer to taking anything for granted.

311. (A) The Yerkes-Dodson law states that difficult tasks are more successful with low arousal and easy tasks are performed better with high arousal. Because simple tasks can be boring, high arousal can keep the person from becoming disengaged.

Chapter 16: Developmental Psychology: Infancy and Childhood

312. (A) Cross-sectional research is a research method used by developmental psychologists because it uses several groups of different-aged individuals who are studied at the same time, saving time and money. Longitudinal research studies the same group of individuals repeatedly at many different points of time.

313. (B) Developmental psychology focuses on the idea that while there are many common patterns to human development, each person's development is also in some ways unique. The combination of shared and distinctive elements is characteristic of all human development. The second theme stresses stability and change. Human development is characterized by both major life transitions and continuities.

314. (B) Damage from teratogens is not always evident at birth but may appear later in life, which is often the case with the teratogen diethylstilbestrol (DES), a synthetic form of the female hormone estrogen linked to various problems later in life, including fertility problems in DES-exposed daughters.

315. (C) Temperament, like personality, is described as the characteristics of a newborn child. Infant temperament has been put into three categories: easy, difficult, and slow-to-warm-up babies. Choice (A) is incorrect because temperament is not necessarily inherited from parents. Choice (B) is incorrect because children are born with a certain temperament; it is not learned. Choice (D) is incorrect because temperament is not modeled behavior. Choice (E) is incorrect because children do not necessarily outgrow temperament.

316. (D) The key word in this question is *all*. The other choices would be correct if the question said "some children." Between 6 and 12 months all babies do acquire depth perception.

317. (A) Choice (A) is the definition of *proximodistal*. *Proximo* in Latin means "near," and *distal* means "far."

318. (C) Choice (C) is the definition of *maturation*. Maturation is a biological process, therefore eliminating choices (A) and (D). Choices (B) and (E) are too vague to clearly define the term.

319. (E) Many students might get confused with choice (D), but the question asks at which stage children are able to grasp the concept of conservation. That would make choice (E) correct. It is during the concrete-operational stage that children are able to grasp those principles.

320. (B) When talking about egocentrism, Piaget believed this concept dealt with preschool-age children. At that age, he believed children do not see things from a different point of view than their own.

321. (A) This stage of cognitive development is usually reached during adolescence. Individuals begin to think in abstract terms. They become capable of going beyond the here and now to understand things in terms of cause and effect.

322. (C) Mary Ainsworth was a developmental psychologist who compared effects of maternal separation, devised patterns of attachment, and observed parent-child attachment.

323. (B) Symbolism is the idea that children can understand that symbols or small objects represent something larger in real life. Children, according to Piaget, can grasp this concept during the preoperational stage, between the ages of two and seven.

324. (A) Depending on age, children assimilate in different ways. An infant sees a block and sucks on it. A toddler sees a block and stacks it or throws it. Adolescents use blocks to play games. Choice (B) could look like the correct answer, but because it only says "thought process," it does not give the exact understanding of the term.

325. (D) According to Lawrence Kohlberg, children in the preconventional stage make decisions based on right or wrong behavior and whether they will be rewarded or punished. Choice (D) uses the term *concrete consequences,* meaning just that.

326. (B) During the conventional stage, adolescents shift their thought process toward considering various abstract social virtues, such as being a good citizen and respecting authority. Some students might get confused with choice (C), postconventional. Postconventional deals more with personal convictions, not necessarily taking into account rules and laws.

327. (C) According to Erik Erikson, during stage 3, initiative versus guilt, a child deals with cognitive development and is expected to meet a new set of challenges. Trust versus mistrust is from birth through the first year of life. Autonomy versus self-doubt is from age one until age three. Industry versus inferiority is from age 5 through age 12. Identity versus role confusion is the adolescent years.

328. (D) Autonomy versus self-doubt, according to Erik Erikson, is between the ages of one and three. It is during this time a child is exploring, walking, and talking, thus beginning the battle of wills with his or her parents. With encouragement, a child will gain a sense of independence. Disapproval brings feelings of doubt.

329. (B) The psychosexual stages are five different developmental periods: oral, anal, phallic, latency, and genital. During these stages an individual seeks pleasure from different areas of the body.

330. (E) Both Sigmund Freud and Erik Erikson believed that if individuals do not solve their problems during each psychosexual or psychosocial stage, problems could arise in the next stage of development.

331. (B) Freud believed that if an individual is fixated in the anal stage, he or she will continue to engage in behaviors that are related to retention. In this case, being overly orderly and stingy are examples of retentive behavior.

332. (A) According to Freud, those individuals fixated in the oral stage can, as adults, become sarcastic and suffer from a low self-esteem, continually looking for approval.

333. (C) According to Lawrence Kohlberg, during the postconventional stage, individuals base their morality on their convictions even if their convictions force them to break the law. Choice (B) could seem like the correct answer, but during the conventional stage, individuals are compelled to follow the law.

334. (D) Choice (A) can be eliminated immediately. Piaget did use different ages for each stage. Choice (B) is incorrect because Piaget was studying cognitive psychology; therefore, he could not have placed too much emphasis on it. Many critics believed Piaget simplified the cognitive abilities of children so much so that he underestimated what they could accomplish.

335. (C) The rooting reflex is seen in normal newborn babies who automatically turn the face toward the stimulus and make sucking, or "rooting," motions with the mouth when the cheek or mouth is touched. The rooting reflex helps to ensure successful breastfeeding.

336. (E) Harry Harlow's work with monkeys and surrogate mothers showed that even monkeys who were deprived of food preferred the terrycloth monkey to the wire monkey with food, demonstrating how important contact and comfort are.

Chapter 17: Developmental Psychology: Adolescence and Adulthood

337. (D) The formal operational stage, Piaget believed, extends from age 11 through adulthood. It is during this stage that adults develop the ability to think abstractly or hypothetically. Adolescents' thoughts about marriage and finding a job in their future is an example of thinking abstractly.

338. (C) According to Kohlberg, conventional morality is used in early adolescence and focuses on upholding laws and rules to gain social approval or maintain social order. Choice (C) is mainly concerned with the social consequences, so it represents conventional morality. Choices (A) and (B) represent preconventional morality, which focuses on self-interest. Choices (D) and (E) represent postconventional morality, which focuses on self-defined ethical principles.

339. (B) Personal fable is when a teenager thinks his or her thoughts are unique to him or her. In this scenario Lola believes no one else could understand how in love she is.

340. (D) Authoritative parents try to encourage their children in a rational and intelligent way. They are supportive, loving, and committed. They have a verbal give-and-take with their children and discuss rules and policies together.

341. (A) The identity versus role confusion stage, according to Erikson, is a time when teenagers have to leave behind the carefree and impulsive behaviors of childhood and develop a purposeful planned adulthood. Choices (B), (C), (D), and (E) all reflect later stages in Erikson's psychosocial stages of development.

342. (C) Passionate love describes an aroused state of intense positive absorption in another person. This state is characteristic of the beginning of a romantic relationship and is associated with higher levels of passion-facilitating hormones like testosterone, dopamine, and adrenaline. As the relationship endures, it will enter a more mature, steady stage known as companionate love. This stage is characterized by a deep, affectionate attachment and higher levels of the hormone oxytocin, which supports feelings of trust, calmness, and bonding.

343. (D) One major criticism of Kohlberg's theory on moral development came from Carol Gilligan. She believed men and women may differ in their moral thinking; men use justice and women use care. Both are socialized differently and, therefore, their moral development will differ greatly.

344. (B) Most psychologists believe that because authoritative parenting involves a give-and-take relationship in which children have a voice, it is the type of parenting that will lead to success in the future.

345. (A) According to Erik Erikson, adolescents are in a stage called identity versus role confusion. Erikson believed that there is a conflict that has to be resolved at every stage in psychosocial development. In this particular stage, if teenagers do not develop an identity they will enter the next stage with role confusion.

346. (B) Many students might feel compelled to choose (C) because the question suggests a reference to the start of preschool. But, in fact, teachers and friends actually become important before preschool. During the initiative versus guilt stage, children are exposed to individuals besides their parents, which is why choice (B) is correct.

347. (D) The number of children one has does not influence how successfully an individual will age. Social-cultural effects that influence aging include support from family and friends, meaningful activities, cultural respect for aging, and safe living conditions. Biological and psychological factors—such as having an optimistic outlook and appropriate nutrition—also influence successful aging.

348. (A) During the industry versus inferiority stage, a child must learn to direct his or her energy toward completing tasks. Teenagers begin to understand the value of success, mainly through report-card grades.

349. (D) Erik Erikson argued that people in their middle adulthood (40–65) are in the stage generativity versus stagnation. Middle adulthood is a time for helping the younger generation. On the negative side, a lack of involvement leads to feelings of stagnation—doing nothing for the younger generation. Choice (C) refers to young adulthood, and choice (E) refers to late adulthood.

350. (C) According to Lawrence Kohlberg, the postconventional stage represents the highest level of moral reasoning. Moral decisions are made after careful thinking about all alternatives and making a balance between human rights and laws of society. Choice (C) is correct because unlike in Kohlberg's other stages of moral development, in the postconventional stage people decide their behavior based on their own morals and values.

351. (E) According to Erik Erikson, young adults are in the intimacy versus isolation stage. If, as an adolescent, you successfully found your own identity you will be ready to find intimacy with a partner by your early twenties. Young adulthood is a time for finding love and a meaningful relationship.

352. (B) The correct pairing in terms of age is choice (B). With all three, an individual is at age 50 or older. The other choices do not correctly correspond with age.

353. (E) Although some students might be tempted to choose (D), latency, the correct answer is genital. The genital stage begins at puberty and goes throughout adulthood. Adolescents would fall under that psychosexual stage.

354. **(C)** According to Freud's psychoanalytic theory, infants are in the oral stage of development. Erikson, who developed a theory of psychosocial stages of development, would say that the infant is in the trust versus mistrust stage of development. Piaget's cognitive development theory places the infant in the sensorimotor stage (the first two years of life).

355. **(D)** Children begin elementary school during the industry versus inferiority stage. Choice (C) might look tempting, but children in that stage are not quite old enough to be in elementary school.

356. **(D)** The social clock refers to the culturally preferred timing of life events and new life stages such as marriage, parenthood, and retirement. The definition of the perceived appropriate time to move away from home, get married, have children, and retire varies from culture to culture and era to era.

Chapter 18: Developmental Psychology: Death and Dying

357. **(B)** According to Erik Erikson, a person in late adulthood (65 and older) is in the integrity versus despair stage of his or her life. It is in this stage that people reflect and review their lives and the choices they made. On the positive side of this stage, if they look back and feel content with their friends and family and how they lived, they feel a sense of satisfaction or integrity.

358. **(A)** According to Elisabeth Kübler-Ross, people go through five stages when dealing with death and grief. Denial is first; anger comes second; bargaining, usually with a higher power, comes third; depression is fourth, and, finally, the last stage is acceptance. Although there are variations to this theory, for the purposes of the AP exam this is the order to know.

359. **(C)** Elisabeth Kübler-Ross formulated a stage theory on death and dying.

360. **(B)** In late adulthood, individuals experience a decline in perceptual speed, reaction time, and processing speed, all of which fall under cognitive abilities. Choice (D) might look enticing, but there is no evidence that people necessarily lose their intellectual ability as they age.

361. **(D)** According to Erik Erikson, an 80-year-old individual is in the integrity versus despair stage. If a person reflects back on his or her life and sees a series of crises, problems, and bad experiences, he or she will have feelings of regret or despair.

Chapter 19: Freudian Psychology

362. **(A)** Freud believed in the importance of the unconscious and that the forces of the unconscious originated in early childhood. Although Freud did study the conscious thought process, most of his work focused on the unconscious. He did not discuss the nature-nurture debate because he believed our personality stems from our environment. This would rule out choices (C) and (D).

363. (C) Freud believed the unconscious motivation explained why we say or do things we can't understand. Unconscious forces represent wishes, desires, or thoughts that, because of disturbing content, we automatically repress.

364. (B) Free association is one of Freud's important discoveries, which is still used today to help reveal a client's unconscious thought process. Choices (A), (C), and (D) can be eliminated because they are not real terms. Choice (E) represents the entire field of Freudian psychology.

365. (C) The id is Freud's first division of the mind. It contains two drives, sex and aggression. Sex and aggression are the source of all mental energy, according to Freud. The ego works to find acceptable ways of satisfying the id's desires. The superego's goal is applying moral values to individual desires.

366. (A) Unlike the ego and id, the superego focuses on the moral values and standards set by one's family, caregivers, and society. Because of this, children learn they must follow rules and regulations.

367. (C) According to Freud, the ego represents the conscious, executive side of the personality that mediates among the demands of the id, superego, and reality. Operating on the reality principle, the ego satisfies the id's desires in realistic ways that will result in pleasure rather than pain.

368. (D) The pleasure principle acts to satisfy wishes or desires and avoid pain while ignoring social regulations. In the case of choice (D), the child acts out because his own wish was not met. The other choices do not show an individual avoiding pain and ignoring society's regulations.

369. (B) Choice (B) is the definition of a defense mechanism. Choices (A), (C), (D), and (E) are all examples of possible defense mechanisms; they do not actually define the term.

370. (E) Sublimation involves redirecting a threatening or forbidden desire, usually sexual, into a socially acceptable one. In this case, Todd puts his sexual frustration into a kickboxing class.

371. (A) Rationalization is the making up of acceptable excuses for behaviors that cause a person to feel anxious. In this case, Jay felt anxious about failing his class and, to reduce his anxiety, made the excuse that his teacher did not like him.

372. (E) Reaction formation involves turning unacceptable wishes into acceptable behaviors. In this case, the fact that Tom is still in love with the woman who broke up with him is an unacceptable behavior. Therefore, he changes his desires into acceptable behavior.

373. (C) According to Freud, the preconscious is the part of the mind that exists right below the surface. It is the connection between the conscious and the unconscious.

374. (D) The phallic stage lasts from about three to six years of age. According to Freud it is a time when children's pleasure seeking is centered on the genitals. This stage is important for personality development because it is a time when boys discover their penis as a source of pleasure. According to Freud boys develop a sexual attraction to their mother and as a result feel jealousy toward their father. This concept became known as the Oedipus complex.

375. (D) The Electra complex was named for Electra, a woman in Greek mythology who killed her mother. Freud theorized that when girls discover they do not have a penis they turn against their mothers and develop sexual desires for their fathers.

376. (E) According to Freud, if a person becomes fixated during the phallic stage he or she may repress sexual urges later in life. Choices (A) and (D) could look like the correct answer, but sexual repression, according to Freud, comes from a fixation during the stage in which children become aware of pleasure from their genitals. During latency all sexual desires are repressed. The genital stage occurs after sexual repression would begin.

377. (A) Many psychologists, including neo-Freudians, did criticize Freud for placing too much emphasis on sexual conflict and the unconscious, and ignoring personal responsibility.

378. (C) The Oedipus complex is a process in which a child competes with the parent of the same sex for the affections and pleasures of the parent of the opposite sex.

379. (B) The id is pleasure seeking, and the superego is highly judgmental. The individual must listen to one of them. Choice (C) could look like the correct answer but because part of Grace's thought process is to keep the money, that is the pleasure-seeking id at work.

380. (E) According to Freud, when a person is fixated in the oral stage, later in life he or she may exhibit behavioral patterns that include choices (A), (B), (C), and (D).

381. (C) According to Freud, men who are fixated in the phallic stage cannot develop the proper relationship with their mothers. This could lead to misogynistic behavior later in life.

Chapter 20: Personality Psychology

382. (A) Archetypes, according to Carl Jung, are universal themes that are part of the collective unconscious. These universal themes are terms or ideas shared by all cultures. Anima, feminine traits; animus, masculine traits; persona, the part of your personality you share publicly; and shadow, the part of your personality you do not publicly share, are all examples of archetypes.

383. (B) The humanistic approach to psychology is concerned with individual potential for growth and the unique perceptions that an individual has in terms of attaining that potential. Humanists believe all humans are born with a need for unconditional positive regard, acceptance, and love from others and themselves in order to achieve their full potential. Psychoanalysis focuses on childhood memories. Cognitive psychology focuses on changing one's thought process. Behavioral psychology focuses on changing one's behavior, and developmental psychology focuses on change versus stagnation.

384. (D) By taking the first letter of each trait, the "Big Five" traits make up the word OCEAN.

385. (B) Generally, type A personality people have more stressful lifestyles. Their fast-paced lifestyle leaves little time for relaxation. Type A personality individuals tend to be in professions that also increase their stress levels. They tend to be perfectionists and will not settle for less. All of these characteristics lead to an increase in potential for cardiac health problems.

386. (C) Carl Jung believed in the archetype called the persona. The persona is the universally shared understanding that people try to bring the best part of their personality to the forefront when in public view. They tend to hide the parts of their personality that they are not comfortable with. In this scenario, George allows the public (his classmates) to see his confidence while hiding his insecurities.

387. (D) The TAT, Thematic Apperception Test, is a projective test in which the subjects are given ambiguous pictures to tell a story about. The MMPI is a test that looks for personality abnormalities. The Rorschach test is an inkblot test. The LSAT is an exam students take to get into law school.

388. (E) Carl Rogers's self theory emphasizes unconditional positive regard for any true, authentic relationship to work. The self theory also places emphasis on congruency, which is when a person's true self, ideal self, and self-image are all congruent with each other. Self-actualization is the ability to reach one's full potential. Empathic understanding is truly understanding and listening to the needs of others. *Extroversion* is the only term that is not part of the self theory.

389. (B) Carl Rogers said that the self is made up of many self-perceptions and personality characteristics. The ideal self is the person whom an individual strives to become, and the real self is the person an individual actually is. These two personas should be consistent with one another.

390. (C) Choice (C) best describes self-efficacy. Many students might get confused with choice (E), but (E) actually defines the term *locus of control*. This term focuses more on whether fate or external causes contribute to our accomplishments.

391. (D) Motivation and determination are examples of internal causes of success. External causes would be putting things in the hands of chance or fate.

392. (D) Factor analysis is used in psychology research to identify factors that explain results of many different tests. It allows researchers to investigate complex concepts that are difficult to measure, such as intelligence or personality, by compressing many variables into a few underlying factors.

393. (B) The trait theory is an approach for analyzing personality structure. It identifies and classifies similarities and differences in personality characteristics. Factor analysis is an actual statistical method to find relationships among different items. Choice (A) can be eliminated because of the use of the word *genetics*. Choice (D) is too vague to be the correct answer. Choice (E) can be eliminated because of the use of the word *behaviors*.

394. (E) The Minnesota Multiphasic Personality Inventory (MMPI) is a true-false questionnaire. The Thematic Apperception Test is a writing test based on ambiguous pictures. The Rorschach test is an inkblot test. Although MMPI is a specific type of objective personality test, choice (D), that is not the best answer.

395. (A) Choice (A) is the only correct answer because it completely negates psychoanalysis and the unconscious by claiming that individuals have free will to reach their full potential.

396. (D) Self-efficacy is different than self-confidence or self-esteem in that it is a subjective expectation of how likely one believes in their ability to succeed at a specific goal or task. Self-efficacy typically varies according to a task or goal. It is also possible to have low self-esteem and yet have high self-efficacy concerning a specific task. Outcome expectancy is belief that a certain behavior is likely to lead to a specific outcome.

397. (D) In contrast to Freud's belief in biological drives, Adler proposed that humans are motivated by social urges and feelings of inferiority. Choice (B) falls under Karen Horney. Choice (C) falls under Carl Rogers. Choice (E) is a learning behavior tool.

398. (B) Karen Horney believed that a major influence on personality development stemmed from the relationship a child had with his or her parents. Unlike Freud's belief in psychosexual conflict, Horney believed these conflicts are avoidable if children are raised in a loving and trusting environment.

399. (A) Attribution theory examines the ways in which people make attributions to a person's behavior, such as internal attribution in which a person is just being difficult and external attribution in which a person is having a bad day due to outside circumstances.

400. (D) One major criticism neo-Freudians had regarding Freud was the emphasis he placed on sexual drives and conflicts in determining our behavior. Neo-Freudians believed much more strongly in our free will to make our own choices.

401. (D) This question clearly defines the humanistic approach.

402. (C) Reciprocal determinism is the idea that a person's behavior both influences and is influenced by personal factors and the social environment. Psychological determinism is the view that people always act upon their greatest drive while rational determinism claims that people act according to their "strongest" or "best" reason. Evolutionary determinism states that evolution and biology play the strongest role in behavioral development while environmental determinism involves the belief that the physical environment affects social and cultural development.

403. (B) Social cognition studies focus primarily on how people process social information, especially its encoding storage, retrieval, and application to social situations. It differs from social psychology, which largely is focused on how people react to the behavior patterns of others during interactive situations. Developmental psychologists study how and why human beings develop over the course of their lives. Behavioral psychologists are concerned with understanding human and animal observable behavior rather than internal events such as thinking.

Chapter 21: Stress and Coping

404. (B) Choice (B) is the definition of the term *stress*. The other choices are all examples of stress but do not give the actual definition.

405. **(C)** A threat appraisal is when the harm or loss has not yet occurred but the individual knows it will happen in the future. Choice (A) occurs when an individual has already sustained some damage or injury. Choice (B) occurs when there is potential for gain or personal growth but it is necessary to mobilize resources in order to achieve success.

406. **(A)** The fight-flight response directs a great amount of energy to the muscles and brain, therefore eliminating choice (B). Threatening physical stimuli trigger the fight-flight response. Choice (C) is incorrect because it does not solely calm the body down. Choice (D) is incorrect because the fight-flight sequence stimulates the pituitary gland, not the thyroid gland. Choice (E) is incorrect because the heart rate is increased first by the fight-flight sequence.

407. **(D)** This answer defines the term *psychosomatic symptoms*.

408. **(B)** The hypothalamus is stimulated when an individual appraises a situation as threatening, psychologically or physically. In turn, the hypothalamus triggers the pituitary gland and simultaneously activates the sympathetic nervous system.

409. **(A)** The adrenal medulla is activated by the sympathetic nervous system. Epinephrine, also known as adrenaline, is released. This hormone increases heart rate, blood pressure, blood flow to muscles, and release of blood sugar. The liver releases glycogen. Acetylcholine is released in both the PNS and CNS, not the adrenal medulla. Serotonin is primarily found in the gastrointestinal tract and the CNS. Dopamine is partially secreted by the hypothalamus, not the adrenal medulla.

410. **(D)** Hans Selye called his theory the general adaptation syndrome. This theory describes the body's reaction to stressful situations. The alarm stage is the initial reaction to stress. The resistance stage is the body's reaction to continued stress. The exhaustion stage is the body's reaction to continuous and long-term stress.

411. **(A)** Frustration is defined as the feeling that results when a person's attempt to reach a goal is blocked. In this scenario, the coach's goal of winning the game was blocked, causing frustration to occur. Choices (B), (D), and (E) could be examples of aggression but not necessarily frustration.

412. **(E)** Choices (B), (C), and (D) are all examples of three different interpretations of a primary appraisal.

413. **(C)** A challenge appraisal is based on one's potential for future success when the proper tools are used. In the example, Eva's professor is letting her know the importance of her success on the tests and quizzes. In other words, the professor is challenging her to do well on them.

414. (B) A harm/loss appraisal implies that an individual has already sustained some injury. A harm/loss appraisal elicits negative emotions such as fear and anxiety, and the individual feels stressed. The more negative emotions, the more stress the individual will have. Choice (D) could seem like the correct answer, but all primary appraisals elicit physiological arousal.

415. (C) During the exhaustion stage, extended periods of stress cause the body to become physically exhausted. Because the body is not meant to handle such strenuous work from the autonomic nervous system, the immune system weakens and there is a breakdown of the internal organs.

416. (A) The alarm stage is the initial reaction to stress. This is when the fight-flight response is activated. In this case, Charlene is entering the initial alarm stage just before the chorus concert starts.

417. (E) Choices (A), (B), (C), and (D) are all examples of the most common triggers of stress. Although fear can cause stress, it is not the major cause of stress for most people.

418. (D) Richard Lazarus's theory emphasized the importance of appraising a situation before experiencing stress.

Chapter 22: Disorders

419. (C) Insanity is legally defined as not knowing right from wrong.

420. (A) The key words from choice (A) associated with the learning perspective are *reinforcement* and *learned behavior*. The learning perspective theorizes that mental disorders are caused from the reinforcement of inappropriate behaviors. Choice (B) would be part of the cognitive perspective. Choice (C) would be part of the psychoanalytic perspective.

421. (C) The Diagnostic Statistical Manual lists common symptoms of psychological disorders. Professionals who classify and diagnose mental disorders use this manual. It does not list the causes of mental disorders, nor does it discuss the treatments.

422. (D) A somatoform disorder is marked by significant bodily symptoms with no physical causes. Although choice (C) might look tempting, individuals with a somatoform disorder do not make up their symptoms. Even though there is no physical cause for their symptoms, they are felt.

423. (E) Obsessive-compulsive disorder consists of persistent obsessive thoughts and irresistible impulses to perform some senseless behavior or ritual. This definition describes the scenario in choice (E).

424. (A) A conversion disorder refers to changing anxiety or emotional stress into real physical or neurological symptoms. In this scenario the soldier turned the psychological horrors of war into a physical symptom of blindness to protect himself.

425. (C) PTSD is listed under Trauma and Stressor-Related Disorders.

426. (B) Generalized anxiety disorder is characterized by excessive worry about almost everything. These anxious feelings can cause irritability and difficulty concentrating.

427. (B) Panic disorder is characterized by unexpected and repeated panic attacks. The symptoms of a panic attack are similar to those described by the patient in this example and can also include trembling, sweating, choking sensations, and heart palpitations.

428. (D) Obsessive-compulsive disorder consists of obsessive, irrational thoughts, impulsive behavior, uncontrollable images, and ritualized behavior. Severe depression is not a symptom of the disorder.

429. (A) A conversion disorder is caused by emotional stress, which turns into physical symptoms with no cause.

430. (A) Selective mutism is a complex childhood anxiety disorder characterized by a child's inability to speak and communicate effectively in select social settings, such as school. These children are able to speak and communicate in settings where they are comfortable, secure, and relaxed. It often coexists with social anxiety disorder. However, a main difference between the two is that in selective mutism the child is unable to talk, while people with social anxiety are typically adolescents or older and "choose" not to talk in certain social situations.

431. (B) Posttraumatic stress disorder can occur after a person has experienced a severely traumatic event such as a car crash. This disorder is characterized by repeatedly reliving the traumatic event through intrusive memories or nightmares, avoidance of places, situations, or people that remind you of the traumatic event, and feeling tense and anxious.

432. (A) Researchers interviewed more than 8,000 individuals between the ages of 15 and 54 years. Almost 50 percent reported having a substance abuse problem at some point in their life. To the surprise of many, substance abuse is considered to be a mental disorder.

433. (E) OCD responds well to cognitive behavioral therapy. This type of therapy coupled with prescribed medication, usually antidepressants or anti-anxiety medications, alleviates the symptoms for most people who suffer from OCD.

434. (A) All subtypes of schizophrenia were removed from the DSM-5 (paranoid, disorganized, catatonic, undifferentiated, and residual).

435. (A) Borderline personality disorder is marked by unstable moods, behavior, and relationships. Dependent personality disorder is when the individual fails to master independence, and hence remains dependent on others for guidance and support. Although the two disorders share common symptoms, a person with BPD responds to fears of abandonment with feelings of rage and emptiness while the person with DPD responds to fear with submissiveness and seeks a new relationship to maintain dependency. Narcissistic personality disorder is a mental disorder in which people have an inflated sense of their own importance, a deep need for admiration, and a lack of empathy for others. Histrionic personality disorder is characterized by a long-standing pattern of attention-seeking behavior and extreme emotionality that often includes wanting to be the center of attention in any group of people. Obsessive-compulsive personality disorder is characterized by a preoccupation with orderliness, perfectionism, and mental and interpersonal control, at the expense of flexibility, openness, and efficiency.

436. (D) Gender-identity disorders involve the desire to become a member of the other sex.

437. (A) Choice (B) is a criteria for avoidant personality disorder. Choices (C) and (D) are old guidelines from DSM-IV. Choice (E) is a criteria for antisocial personality disorder in DSM-IV.

438. (A) Gender dysphoria is a new classification for the now defunct diagnosis of gender identity disorder. Homosexuality was declassified as a mental disorder in 1973. Hysterical neurosis was deleted in the 1980 DSM-III. Delusional disorders remain in DSM-V.

Chapter 23: Mood Disorders and Schizophrenia

439. (E) Schizophrenia is not a mood disorder. A mood disorder is characterized as a prolonged and disturbed emotional state that affects an individual's thoughts and behaviors. Schizophrenia is a serious mental disorder with symptoms such as delusions and hallucinations.

440. (C) Dysthymic disorder is characterized by being chronically depressed for a period of two years.

441. (D) There is a direct link between levels of serotonin in the body and the onset of depression.

442. (A) Choice (A), major depression, is the only choice that is not a characteristic of a personality disorder. Major depression fits under mood disorders.

443. (B) This scenario describes a psychopath. Disregard for others, random violence, continuous lying, and little remorse are all symptoms of being a psychopath.

444. (B) Fear or avoidance of situations in which escape might be difficult or help unavailable when panic strikes is characteristic of agoraphobia. Although major depressive disorder can cause someone to lose interest in activities they used to find pleasurable, fearful avoidance of certain activities and situations is not a key symptom.

445. (E) Individuals with paranoid personality disorder suffer from distrust and suspicion of others. They tend to assume that other people have evil tendencies or motives.

446. (B) Dissociative identity disorder (DID) is the presence of two or more identities or personality states. Each one has its own thought process and relation to the world. Much research has been done regarding DID. One explanation is a severe trauma from childhood, specifically abuse, which causes the mental split or dissociation of identities as a way of defending or coping with the memories of the trauma.

447. (A) The major indicator that Scott is suffering from antisocial personality disorder is the lack of remorse for his poor behavior.

448. (D) Unlike major depression or dysthymic disorder, individuals with bipolar disorder will go through several days or weeks with depression and then become manic. In this scenario, Priscilla shows her manic behavior by taking her life savings to spend on a shopping spree in Europe.

449. (B) The dopamine theory of schizophrenia says that the level of the neurotransmitter dopamine is overactive in schizophrenic patients, causing a wide range of symptoms. On the other hand, people who suffer from Parkinson's disease actually have low levels of the neurotransmitter dopamine.

450. (D) Manic behavior is not a symptom of schizophrenia. The other choices are all commonly seen symptoms of schizophrenia.

451. (A) Type I schizophrenia includes having positive symptoms, such as hallucinations, which is a distortion of normal functioning. The other choices are all examples of negative emotion, which means the sympathetic nervous system slows down.

452. (E) Personality disorders impair people's ability to function in society without depression or delusions. They are characterized by inflexible, enduring, and disruptive behaviors. Antisocial personality disorder is the most severe and heavily researched of the personality disorders.

453. (B) Dissociative fugue is marked by a sudden inability to recall one's own past. The person may not remember his or her identity. Choice (A) might look like a tempting answer, but dissociative amnesia is usually associated with a stressful or traumatic event, physically or psychologically. Choice (C), dissociative identity disorder, is also known as multiple personality disorder, which has nothing to do with memory loss.

454. (E) When testing a genetic marker or a genetic link, researchers must use identical twins because they share 100 percent of the same genetic makeup.

455. (B) Major depression is linked to below-normal levels of serotonin. Although there is evidence that below-normal dopamine levels also affect depression, choice (A) says moderate levels, not below-normal levels.

456. (A) Developmental disorders are first diagnosed in early childhood or adolescence. Autism falls under this label because its diagnosis is made in early childhood.

457. (D) Narcissists absolutely suffer from an inflated sense of self. Some students might want to put choice (A) as the answer, but that is not necessarily true for narcissists, more so for individuals suffering with borderline personality disorder.

Chapter 24: Therapies

458. (C) This question uses the term *past experiences*, which corresponds directly to psychoanalytic therapy and past conflict.

459. (B) Insight therapy focuses on identifying the causes of the client's problems. Once the client has an insight into the cause of the problem, possible solutions are discussed.

460. (A) Unlike a clinical psychologist, a psychiatrist is a medical doctor and can therefore prescribe medication using biomedical treatment.

461. (E) Client-centered therapy helps the client assume a self-actualizing state. This therapy empowers the client to reach his or her full potential. With the use of positive regard, the client feels encouraged to take charge of the therapy session.

462. (A) Prozac is part of a category of drugs that work as selective serotonin reuptake inhibitors. In other words, serotonin becomes more available in the body, helping those who suffer from depression.

463. (C) Rational emotive therapy (RET) is a cognitive therapy that focuses on reconstructing the client's self-defeating ways of thinking.

464. (B) Choice (B) is the definition of *aversive therapy*. Aversive therapy basically uses a stimulus-response approach to rid an individual of negative behavior.

465. (D) Most people associate dream analysis with psychoanalysis. Gestalt therapy also includes dream analysis, which helps to look at the whole picture of an individual's conflict.

466. (A) Transference is a Freudian belief that describes a client-therapist relationship. In this process the client transfers emotions and substitutes the therapist for someone important in the client's life.

467. (A) Cognitive therapy, as developed by Aaron Beck, assumes that we have automatic negative thoughts that we continually say to ourselves. By using these thoughts we actually distort our perception of the world.

468. (B) Systematic desensitization is a behavioral technique that gradually exposes a client to a specific feared object while simultaneously practicing relaxation techniques.

469. (D) The humanistic approach is built on the importance of empathy and support. Behavioral therapies are sometimes criticized for being too mechanical. The humanistic approach focuses most on unconditional positive regard.

470. (C) Rational emotive therapy, according to Albert Ellis, works to rid the client of negative thoughts, which are impeding his or her achievement of life goals.

471. (A) Free association is a technique that encourages the client to talk about any thoughts or images that enter his or her head. This free-flowing talk is supposed to provide material from the unconscious.

472. (E) The presence of the disorder is correlated with reduced levels of light, which accompanies the onset of winter. Controlled exposure to artificial light is often successful in treating seasonal affective disorder.

473. (A) Self-actualization is associated with the humanistic approach, not psychoanalysis.

474. (A) Aaron Beck developed a kind of cognitive therapy that specifically focused on ridding individuals of the negative thoughts that prevent them from achieving their goals.

475. (D) This statement specifically defines the term *biofeedback*. The key word that can help an individual answer this question correctly is *feedback*. Feedback refers to an individual, in this case the client, receiving immediate information.

476. (C) Behavioral therapy is used in treating anxiety disorders through systematic desensitization therapy. Behavioral therapy is used to help individuals with autism through positive reinforcement. Behavioral therapists work with drug addicts to try to find what triggers their addictive tendencies.

Chapter 25: Social Psychology

477. (C) Researchers have analyzed group decision-making processes involved in making bad decisions, such as the Bay of Pigs. They discovered something called "groupthink." This occurs when group discussions emphasize sticking together to make the "best" decision. There is usually one member who discourages ideas that might threaten group unity. In the Bay of Pigs situation, many of John F. Kennedy's advisors did just that.

478. (B) Ethnocentrism describes the belief that one's own culture or ethnic group is superior.

479. (B) Self-serving bias refers to explaining our successes by attributing them to our dispositions or personality traits and attributing our failures to the situation.

480. (A) Philip Zimbardo's "mock prison" experiment in the early 1970s is extremely important to know for the AP exam. He was interested in studying group dynamics in prison. He got student volunteers to play the roles of prisoners and prison guards. The volunteers became immersed in their roles, and many of the "guards" conformed so much to what was expected of their role that they began to punish and humiliate the volunteers who played the roles of powerless inmates.

481. (D) Choice (D) basically defines the term *cognitive dissonance*. Essentially, we strive to keep our behaviors and attitudes consistent with one another. Leon Festinger coined this term to describe the internal tension when our behavior and attitude do not mesh.

482. (A) Ethnocentrism is the assumption that your culture is superior to other cultures. The assumption that your culture's cuisine is the best is an example of ethnocentrism. Choices (B) and (E) describe discrimination, negative behavior aimed at a group and its members. Choices (C) and (E) represent prejudices, negative attitudes toward a group and its members.

483. (C) Stanley Milgram originally developed this experiment to try to better understand the answer many Nazi soldiers gave in the Nuremberg trials. Milgram's experiment deals specifically with obedience to authority figures.

484. (E) Collectivist cultures emphasize the needs and goals of the group over the individual. In these types of cultures, relationships with other group members and the interconnectedness between people are important factors in each person's identity. Therefore, a collectivist culture would not be likely to emphasize the importance of self-sufficiency.

485. (D) The diffusion of responsibility theory says that in the presence of others, individuals feel less personal responsibility and are less likely to take action in a situation where help is required.

486. (B) The fundamental attribution error refers to our tendency, when looking for a cause of a person's behavior, to focus on the person's disposition and ignore or overlook the situational reasons.

487. (E) Part of Asch's results showed that individuals are less likely to conform in certain situations; one is if there is just one other person who does not conform in the group.

488. (C) Group cohesion is simply group togetherness, which is determined by how much group members perceive that they share common attributes, goals, and values.

489. (C) Peripheral route persuasion is a way to influence the beliefs of others. It uses incidental cues—such as an endorsement by a famous actor—to persuade people. This method does not use logic or systematic thinking but instead relies on people making fast, snap judgments. In contrast, central route persuasion uses evidence and logical arguments to persuade already-interested or naturally analytical people.

490. (C) Compliance is a kind of conformity in which we give in to social pressure in our public responses but do not change our private beliefs.

491. (D) Deindividuation states that we are more likely to behave out of character when there are high levels of anonymity and low probability of getting caught. Choice (E) might look correct, but that is actually an example of diffusion of responsibility.

492. (A) Using specific dilemmas, researchers compared the recommendations from individuals in a group with those made by the group after it had engaged in discussion. Group discussions change individuals' judgments, such as when groups urge a riskier recommendation than do individuals.

493. (B) Groupthink occurs when group discussions emphasize sticking together with an agreement over the use of critical thinking. This situation creates an "in group" and an "out group." Allowing all group members the freedom to share their opinions can eliminate groupthink.

494. (D) In this scenario, Randy believes he personally works harder than others, attributing his success to his own disposition. While choice (E) might look enticing, just because Rebi overestimates her ability to run a program does not mean she is attributing her success to her own disposition.

495. (D) Individualistic cultures place a priority on individual goals over the needs and goals of the group. People in these cultures tend to be independent and autonomous. Social behavior is heavily influenced by the preferences of the individual. As a result, individuals are not defined by their relationships to others, but instead by their uniqueness.

496. (B) Because the question asked what the dissonance theory would state, David would have to change one of his beliefs in order to reduce his cognitive inconsistencies.

497. (B) Although choice (D) might look like the correct answer, it is not specific enough to this scenario. The actor-observer bias occurs when a person judges other people's behavior based on their personal attributes and the person's own behavior based on the situation.

498. (B) Although many people believe in the notion that opposites attract, the reality is that individuals tend to date and marry people similar to themselves in terms of morals, values, and life perspectives.

499. (D) The just-world hypothesis is the belief that good people do good things and bad people do bad things. To understand why an individual was raped, the just-world hypothesis would cause a person to assume the victim "asked for it."

500. (E) This scenario defines the concept of social facilitation, which is the increase in performance in the presence of a crowd.

501. (C) Diffusion of responsibility is the idea that in the presence of others, individuals feel less personal responsibility and are less likely to take action in a situation where help is required.